*Call Yourself
a Manager!*

Call Yourself
a Manager!

MATTHEW ARCHER

MERCURY BOOKS
Published by W.H. Allen & Co. Plc

First published March 1987
Reprinted January 1988
Published by the Mercury Books Division of
W.H. Allen & Co. Plc
44 Hill Street, London W1X 8LB

Typeset in Meridien by
Phoenix Photosetting, Chatham, Kent
Printed and bound in Great Britain by
Mackays of Chatham Ltd, Chatham, Kent

Cartoons by Andrew Birch

British Library Cataloguing in Publication Data

Archer, Matthew
    Call yourself a manager.
    1. Management   2. Business
    I. Title
    658   HD31

ISBN 1–85252–000–0

INTRODUCTION

Throughout the business world there are thousands of people trying desperately hard to become 'a manager'. Some of those who have made it to a management position have aspirations to become the 'chief executive'.

The reasons for wishing to become a manager are many and varied, including status, security, megalomania and money. There was one aspiring executive who gave his reason for wishing to be a manager as the opportunity to push other people around as he had been pushed around for a number of years!

The supreme problem, having achieved the title of manager, is how to behave like one. Management, particularly at top level, is one of the most difficult and demanding jobs – and one where perfection is impossible to attain.

It is not too difficult to acquire the technical knowledge (e.g. engineering, sales technique, mathematics) that goes with the job but the human element is much more elusive. Managers, being human (at least most of them), are subject to their own emotional and other weaknesses. Their performance can be affected by their fears, prejudices, lifestyle and relationships with others, such as subordinates, colleagues and outsiders, who are also affected by fears, prejudices and so on. They are also subject to the politics of business and the professional mysteries of specialists such as computer programmers, accountants and lawyers.

The manager can find himself (or herself) battling all at once with a rebellious workforce that just will not understand the facts, a chief accountant who persists in pressing incomprehensible financial points, a feeling that he is somehow not looking after his budget properly and a fellow manager who attacks him at every possible opportunity. All in all, a fairly ghastly prospect which makes one wonder why anyone wants to be a manager at all!

The fact is that the majority of people who become managers receive no training in advance and are blissfully unaware of the agonies that lie ahead. Having become, usually painfully, aware of these agonies, many managers will seek an easy way out. While very few opt for a self-inflicted bullet in the brain, many turn a blind eye to the demands of their jobs.

It is entirely possible for a manager to go through his or her career ignoring many of the responsibilities of the job – even ending up as chief executive – without ever having fully managed at all. Some take such a way out knowingly. Others, like the workaholic, are entirely unaware that they are ducking their responsibilities and, indeed, will argue that their dedication and hard work is proof of their conscientiousness.

This book deals with some of those requirements of management which come as a surprise to those who arrive untrained at management level and may be painful to those who prefer to ignore the problems, hoping they will go away. The manager who takes refuge in committees and meetings, the manager who shelters behind his ignorance or prejudices and the manager who dedicates himself to an obsession with pointless accuracy are all commented on.

It is certainly true that the manager who identifies, accepts and teaches himself to handle the problems will not only be a better manager but will enjoy his working life much more. To those who wish to achieve this enjoyment this book is dedicated.

Business students may find the book an entertaining

supplement to the tougher items on their reading lists and, at the other end of the scale, chief executives should find something of particular relevance to their personal policy and philosophy. The contents are based on real-life experience and all the examples are real – if disguised. It is fervently hoped that every reader will find the contents thought-provoking.

The notations he/she, his/hers, etc., being cumbersome to read, have been kept to a minimum. Unless the context otherwise dictates, the gender used should be read as including both sexes.

CONTENTS

1

THE COMPLEAT MANAGER

A consultant was discussing various problems with a sales manager in charge of a team of six salesmen. The manager was asked how he defined his job:

'To get some work out of these bastards,' was his reply.

The sales manager was absolutely serious about this simple definition and could see no other function for which he was responsible. This man, formerly a very successful salesman, had been promoted to sales manager without any training in management skills. It had not occurred to him that he might assume a responsibility to teach his subordinates some of the skills that had enabled him to succeed as a salesman himself. To have done so would, in view of the commission arrangements, have been in his own financial interest, but this had apparently escaped his notice. Nor did he recognise any other responsibilities inherent in his job, such as planning the work of his team and ensuring that they contributed to his company's profitability. He was nothing more than a 'driver' who had been born too late. His singleminded approach would have made him a first-class master of a slave galley.

Many (perhaps most) managers take a narrow, parochial view of their jobs. By excluding many of the more tiresome responsibilities, they can make life more bearable. A limited range of responsibilities makes life simpler. Unfortunately a

nice, simple life is unlikely to be the lot of the truly professional manager, who must recognise, accept and practise a
wide range of activities in order to achieve his objectives. He
must also recognise, and be able to cope with, the attitudes of
other managers.

Another sales manager, of milder temperament, was
equally narrow in his approach. His answer to a similar
question regarding his role was 'To give service to customers'.

At first glance such a definition might seem reasonable.
However, further consideration gives rise to doubts as to
what was implied. A customer can always be given service *at
a price*. A warehouse expensively stocked with every
variation of product might be part of the service. Delivery
(by chartered jet) of every nut or bolt urgently required
might be another. In other words, this man's anxiety to keep
his customers happy might bankrupt the company.

Incidentally, the production boss of the same company
was asked how he saw his role. His reply was: 'If I can keep
the bloody sales department off my back, my life is more
bearable. I keep the warehouse as full as possible. What they
don't realise is that the demands for small quantities of
"specials" interrupts production runs and reduces output'.
The production man's role had been reduced to one of main-
taining high stocks (at any cost) as a result of the sales manager's simple wish to give service (at any cost).

None of these managers showed any concern for their
human resources or with the prosperity of the business.
Their single-minded approach was paramount and this was
obviously not working to the good of the firm.

To achieve optimum profits and maintain a sensible balance between the costs of each function it is essential that
each department works to a plan. This plan will set limits to
the actions of department heads – directing them through
programmes which are complementary, minimising waste
and achieving the best possible performance for the firm *as a
whole*.

Perhaps one explanation for dedication to a narrow

objective lies in the attitude behind a remark heard in a hotel corridor. Two managers attending a fairly intensive course on management skills were discussing the work done so far. One manager commented that he was surprised how much there was to management. The other replied: 'I find all this management business quite fascinating but too difficult . . . Actually I don't think I want anything to do with it'!

If these attitudes are in any way typical, they are also more than a little frightening to anyone trying to run a business. Drucker in his book *The Practice of Management* says that the manager is the 'dynamic life giving element' in the business. Without a manager's leadership the resources of production remain as resources and never actually become production. If 'managers' want nothing to do with management, then the company is doomed.

Drucker also maintains that the best definition of management is provided by examining the manager's role. Many managers, at seminars and courses, have asked for a definition of management (or administration as some people like to call it). They have in many cases been seeking a simple one-line statement. No such simple definition exists, and it is indeed necessary to look at the manager's role and spell it out in full.

A definition in terms of the manager's role reveals two levels of responsibility or prime function but with both levels requiring similar skills:

1 *The top management role.* This role deals with policy decisions concerning the objectives of the organisation and the conduct of its affairs. For example, what sort of business are we going to operate? (Clock-making? Hotels? Franchise?). Where are we going to operate? (Worldwide? Europe? London? The regions?). How will the business be organised? What return on capital do we expect?, etc.

2 *The middle and lower management role.* This concerns decisions regarding methods. For example, *how* will operations be organised? What level of output is needed in

order to meet the demands of top management? How can this output be economically achieved? These decisions must then be translated into action – in short, middle and lower management has to produce results to meet the requirements of the policy-makers. In order to produce results, managers must work effectively with the resources at their disposal. The main resources are people. The manager, therefore, must work through the people to get the results. The more effectively the manager uses (i.e. leads) them, the more easily will he be able to produce the required results.

Effective use of human resources comprises:

Selection of staff
Training and development of staff
Communication with staff
Planning and organising work
Control of results
Motivation of staff

In order to meet these demands the manager needs certain personal qualities combined with executive and technical skills. The personal qualities, which result from education, character and various influences over the years include such features as:

Approachability (Sorry, but there seems to be no better word)
Sensitivity to others and their feelings
Flexibility of outlook
Balance and maturity
Ability to think logically and clearly
Dependability

These characteristics should be present in sufficient measure for a manager to be able to adopt a more constructive and sophisticated role than merely 'getting some work out of the bastards'.

The executive skills will include:

Ability to communicate (which includes listening)
Ability to co-operate
Ability to make decisions

These may sound very obvious but there are many managers who can give orders but cannot communicate. They are often the same ones who regard co-operation as loss of a battle. There are also far too many managers unwilling or unable to make decisions. It is not suggested that all decisions should be made on the spur of the moment. The trick is to find a balance between impulsive decisions and thinking it over into infinity.

Technical skills consist of:

A good background of commercial and industrial practice
A good knowledge of the business
Specialist knowledge of the work of the manager's own unit
Ability to organise and control
Ability to select and use management techniques.

So, to be a manager in anything more than name is asking quite a lot. However, with the qualities and skills listed he should, with a measure of flair and commonsense, be able to achieve – and help his staff to achieve. In other words, he will be a leader. Successive chapters deal with some of the leadership problems which can arise (including some of the less easily defined problems) within the context of the factors stated above.

Action checklist

1 Accept the fact that true management requires the practice of a wide range of skills and involvement in many areas of activity.

2 Identify the knowledge and skills required, acquire them and put them into practice.
   The first step is to identify any 'areas' which can be improved. This can be done by self-assessment (no embarrassing exposure to colleagues is necessary!)

Use a simple tick-chart as follows:

Attribute	Poor	Fair	Average	Good
Technical know-how				
Relations with staff				
Relations with other managers				
Flexibility				
Ability to make decisions				
. . . and so on				

Note: do not leave out any of the essential attributes and do not cheat!

3 Refer to the Appendix on page 121 for sources of help in cases where anything less than *Good* has been ticked.

2

THE CHIEF EXECUTIVE

This species of manager comes in two forms – very good and dreadful. There seems to be nothing in between.

Assuming that the 'Peter Principle' is right, i.e. that we are all promoted to our level of incompetence, it is not unreasonable to argue that the majority of chief executives should be fairly useless. They, after all, represent the ultimate in promotion. Incompetence can often be confirmed by observation and seems to be the experience of many people in business. Grumbling about the chief executive is a widespread activity.

It can also be argued that the nature of an organisation is largely determined by the nature and abilities of the men or women at the top. This is particularly marked in the smaller companies, where the chief executive's influence is less diluted by sheer numbers and layers of people.

So, it is vital for the health of a business, and the people in it, that the chief executive is a good manager – with all that is implied by the term. What in fact do we find? See if you can recognise any of the following types, all of which are taken from real life although sometimes more than one individual has been combined under each heading.

Types of chief executive

The big tycoon
This CE is often a workaholic (see Chapter 6) but at the very

least is obsessively dedicated and very demanding. He wants a finger in every pie and will never let his minions (which is how he sees them) get on with their jobs in peace.

He skips his holidays and works through his weekends. One CE was known to disappear on holiday on Friday night only to reappear on the following Monday morning announcing that he was bored with his holiday. He would rejoin his family two weeks later to bring them home again!

The big tycoon is often a very clever man (but not necessarily intelligent), blessed with an enormous capacity for work. Armed with these characteristics, he can often produce the results. However, it is a dangerous situation.

His style causes great tension in his subordinates and the better ones become frustrated and angry. They depart for more satisfying jobs elsewhere, leaving the lesser mortals behind. Thus one finds the big tycoon supported by a team characterised by dedicated mediocrity (with a sprinkling of sycophants for good measure). Such people are useless when the big tycoon retires or goes into cardiac arrest. After his departure the business goes to pieces.

The spent bullet

The Peter Principle personified, this CE was very good at a lower level but is now so out of his depth that he cannot even decide what his job is. He is too proud to ask anyone else to define his role for him (e.g. a consultant, a business school professor, or even his colleagues) so he opts out.

He becomes bored and joins the gin-and-tonic circuit, having discovered that he can justify his existence by pretending to be 'the company's ambassador'. This comprises lots of golf, 'working' lunches with other spent bullets and long days at conferences and exhibitions.

He loses touch with the guts of the business and is unable to contribute usefully when a crisis occurs. One such man made a point of discovering an urgent necessity to make a foreign trip whenever there was need to grapple with a difficult problem.

If he is lucky, the spent bullet will have a loyal and conscientious second in command who will, despite some resentment, pick up the ball and carry it for him. If not, the business will drift – perhaps into oblivion. Alternatively, the vacuum he leaves may be filled by two or three able and ambitious men who will spend a lot of energy fighting each other to gain control, which can be a serious waste of effort and talent.

The specialist

This CE arrives at the top with experience of only one aspect of the business. Sales or accounting seem to be the most popular areas. He is probably a product of a business organised on functional lines, which has prevented him from gaining first-hand experience of any aspect of the business outside his own functional area.

Thus we find the CE who has been, successively, accounts clerk, junior accountant, accountant, chief accountant and financial director. He may have had a death-defying excursion into auditing at some stage as well. Whatever the case, we have a CE who is at the same time the most experienced bookkeeper in the firm and the least experienced businessman. He will look at every problem only in terms of pounds and pence, finding it difficult to consider the customer's or the employee's viewpoint. The company will ossify through lack of entrepreneurial thinking and will probably be a singularly boring company to work for.

The sales-oriented CE will be a much more exciting character but he will put the financial stability of the company in jeopardy. As soon as he is appointed, he will find himself in a perfect position to please his pet customers. All his old buddies from days of yore will ring him up, knowing that he will instantly promise them the earth. Ridiculous delivery dates will be agreed, spurious complaints met with credit notes, and costly one-off special production jobs given priority over bread and butter lines. One such fortunate customer was kept going for more than a year with free 'sample quantities'!

All this will be justified on the grounds of customers being 'the life blood of the business' or 'service to customers is the only advantage we have over the opposition'. These arguments are difficult to counter, as they are often essentially true. The sales-oriented CE, however, *extends* their truth to justify *any* action, however damaging.

Internally, the sales-oriented CE will cause alarm and despondency on the production side. For years the production director and his team have fought him to maintain a balance in production planning – or to maintain production planning at all. The CE has long regarded the production team as a rather grubby-handed bunch of obstructionists who cannot see the obvious commercial necessities of the business. Now, by thunder, he will sort them out! Which is precisely why morale and enthusiasm on the production side will be replaced by a strong defensive posture and deep suspicion.

No doubt production-oriented CEs also exist and no doubt they are as blinkered as the other specialists.

The hedonist

This CE was formerly a well balanced and reasonable character who limited his physical indulgence in accordance with the need to have his expense claims approved by someone else. Now he has reached the top, there is no one to check him and, often gradually, he becomes more and more lavish with the company's money.

His consumption of booze steadily increases – probably as a result of practice gained at the more numerous lunches and other functions he attends. He will also be tempted to keep up with the Joneses from other companies and he will match their spending at certain 'executive clubs' to be found in London's West End, mid-town Manhattan and elsewhere.

This leads to the deadly combination of birds and booze. A very expensive and exhausting mixture!

Some of the hedonists acquire a taste for luxurious offices (more keeping up with the Joneses) and expensive limousines complete with heavily underemployed chauffeurs whose jobs are much sought after. The chauffeur enjoys an easy day, combined with hefty overtime payments resulting from waiting around in the evenings to take the boss back to his company flat. At least one chauffeur was reputed to be given a share of the birds and booze from time to time.

It is not necessary to be a puritan to condemn such behaviour and one may even say 'good luck' to the CE who gets his kicks this way. But as a manager he runs the risk of becoming too seduced by the 'good life' to have sufficient time and energy for the business. He also risks upsetting his colleagues, who will see what he is doing – especially if, as one hedonist CE used to do, he boasts about his pleasures to his underlings.

There is just too great a risk of diminished performance and loss of confidence to permit approval of the hedonist. Apart from that, he is spending the shareholders' money.

The water closet

This is the man who is flushed with enthusiasm every so often. Most of the time he is closeted in his office apparently dormant. He is most difficult to deal with, since, for long periods, he gives no indication of what he wants to do, wants to hear or wants other people to do.

Suddenly one day he emerges from his office and launches into activity. This can take the form of a visit to a factory, a personal investigation into the company communications systems (he has just read an article in the *Financial Times* about word-processors or microcomputers) or simply an expedition to 'stir things up a bit'.

This CE, possibly a variant of the 'spent bullet', can do a lot of harm. During his dormant period he is out of touch. No one tells him anything and he does not ask. The result is that his enthusiasms are usually irrelevant and disruptive. Much time is wasted by all and sundry in justifying their positions, collecting facts or keeping out of the way.

The sad thing is that in due course the enthusiasm wears off and the CE retires to his office for a further dormant period – having achieved nothing. Nothing, that is, except to create urgent work which has taken priority over the important work.

One such CE suddenly demanded to know certain information from the many branches of his company. This information was not recorded as a matter of routine and was difficult and expensive to collect. Whilst the collection process was going on, an O & M analyst happened to call at a regional office where he found the regional boss in an agitated state. The boss told the analyst of the CE's demands and how difficult and time-consuming it was to obtain the data. He was also, and this is important, doubtful if the data he was collecting was accurate.

The analyst asked him if there was any way in which the collected data could be checked and he replied that it could not. He also stated that he had answers from about ten of his thirty or so branches and the answers were closely similar in each. The analyst suggested that he call off the hunt and give 'guesstimate' figures for the remaining branches at about the same magnitude as the first ten. He gave this advice because he strongly suspected that the resulting information could be of no practical value to the company.

This was later confirmed to be true. The CE had asked for the information 'as a matter of interest' and not to make a decision or to influence any particular course of action.

There were about 250 branches in all and twelve regional offices. The work required in each was about 1 man/day. Thus, the 'matter of interest' cost the company about 260 man-days' work to produce figures which were of dubious accuracy in the first place.

Another damaging characteristic of the 'water closet' is his tendency to 'take over' something from his subordinates. A project or job well under control, and probably the proud interest of a departmental manager, is suddenly subject to direction (interference) from the CE. The manager hitherto running the show is naturally put out by the interference and his reactions can include one or more of the following:

(a) He doesn't trust me.

(b) He thinks it is too important for me to handle and I am now being made to lose status.
(c) I have done all the work so far and he (the CE) is going to take all the glory.
(d) If he wants to do it let him – I won't help if he makes a mess of it.
(e) I hope he makes a mess of it.

Whatever the reaction may be, it is invariably bad for the company, the subordinate and the CE.

The patron

This CE is often excellent in many ways except that he tends to favouritism. The CE's patronage is extended to some fortunate individual who can do no wrong. This individual can be regarded, in the style of ancient Rome, as a 'client', since the Roman phenomenon of Patron and Client is closely paralleled in the modern business situation. However, the good fortune of the client is normally of limited duration because of the following:

(a) The patron becomes disenchanted and switches his favour elsewhere.
(b) The client is assassinated by his jealous colleagues.

One senior man favoured a young man and gave him rapid promotion. He also regarded his secretary as worthy of better things. The young man was promoted well beyond his abilities and the secretary given an executive role. The other staff saw this as reward for years of sycophantic service not justified by ability.

The last that was heard of them they were sinking fast, with their colleagues (especially those overlooked for promotion) gleefully doing all they could to bring them down. Their patron will of course do all he can to rescue his clients, until he becomes aware that their failings are reflecting badly on himself. Then he will get rid of or abandon them as quickly as possible! The energy consumed by such situations would be far better employed on profit-making activities –

most of which take second place when favouritism and jealousy rear their heads.

Patronage is often linked with social and sporting activities. A senior man, stating that young Snooks had done very well for the cricket team, appointed him to a certain committee. The committee appointment was a prestigious one and demanded skills which had absolutely no connection with the cricket field. The result was a series of embarrassments and anger as the committee struggled to carry the sporting passenger.

A more amusing story concerned the farewell presentation party for a retiring managing director. After the usual speeches and drinks one of the old stagers in the company began to reminisce about former managing directors (this was in a quiet corner and was not part of the official proceedings). His reminiscences went something like this:

> The first MD I knew was old Bumblethorpe. He was a keen golfer and everyone who wanted to get on in the firm had to spend many hours plodding round the golf course. Postlethwaite came next, and he was a drinking man. Half the managers put their livers at risk keeping up with him. Then came Fothergill, who was a sailing fanatic. We spent many miserable evenings and weekends soaked to the skin and feeling sick.
>
> Then came this chap and as I said at the time 'Heaven help us if this one is a sword swallower!'

By way of contrast to all these top level disasters, one of the best CEs is worth describing. He was not perfect but then none of us are. His virtues easily outweighed his faults, resulting in a leader who achieved excellent results for his shareholders and admiration from his staff. His main characteristics were as follows:

1 A very sound knowledge of the business and the technical content of its major parts.
2 Hard work balanced by an ability to relax.

3 Accessibility to colleagues at all levels (his door *was* always open – given reasonable notice).

4 A friendly democratic manner – no one was beneath his notice.

5 A willingness to listen – however busy he was. He also 'suffered fools gladly'.

6 Ability to monitor and supervise without interfering.

7 Willingness to delegate and to give younger, less experienced staff a chance.

8 Acceptance of his responsibilities – and blame when things went wrong.

9 Fairness (which was seen) and total absence of favouritism.

10 A keen sense of humour.

This CE kept his finger on the pulse by attending the board meetings of the subsidiaries within the group and by means of carefully chosen information from regular reports. Routine and ad hoc briefing sessions were held, including first-hand reports of operations from levels below his immediate subordinates.

This latter technique was very skilfully used in a way which nevertheless demonstrated that he was not usurping the powers of other directors. All such reporting was by mutual agreement and never in secret. There was, however, one occasion on which he held a 'secret' meeting. The facts of this instance give much food for thought.

A middle-aged but junior employee was suddenly dismissed. The CE heard about it and asked the personnel manager what lay behind it. The personnel manager explained that the man had stolen some money from the company and dismissal was inevitable. The CE then arranged to see the dismissed employee and they talked alone for about two hours. When the meeting was over, the employee was reinstated in his job and the CE had a talk with the personnel manager.

The gist of the latter talk was that the employee, who had loyally served the company for many years, had committed an act which, although quite wrong, was uncharacteristic. The CE had ascertained that the man had suffered considerable problems in his private life and was under great strain. He was now reinstated with a promise of help from the company and an arrangement for him to pay back the stolen money by monthly instalments.

Some people saw this as the end of all discipline in the company. Others saw it as justice tempered with mercy. At all events the company had gained a *very* loyal employee and had got its money back!

The lesson was not lost on those employees who heard the story. If in trouble, it was not necessary to steal from the company. The company would help them.

Perhaps such humanity and flexibility of mind were additional reasons why this man was so successful in his job.

The chief executive and the state visit

From time to time CEs have to make 'state visits' to one of the further flung parts of their empires. The annual visit is made to the factories or a branch office or perhaps an overseas subsidiary.

This is a great opportunity for a CE to encourage, motivate and learn. Unfortunately it often does not work out that way. It is not unknown for a CE to let it be seen that he is bored and fed up with the whole process and would much rather be back in his comfortable office than plodding round a noisy and dirty factory.

Some state visits are characterised by a stupendous lack of sensitivity to local feelings and one such case occurred in an engineering company. It was announced to the workforce that the managing director would be visiting the factory on a particular day and would be inspecting the various workshops. Despite some cynical comment from the barrack-room lawyers, most of the employees were pleased at the prospect. They were proud of their work and were flattered that the great man was coming to see it.

Workshops and equipment were tidied up and cleaned. The car park was swept and tablecloths provided for the canteen (someone presumed that he would stop for a cup of tea).

The big day arrived and 'the buzz' went round the factory that the visitor and entourage had arrived. The visiting party made its way to the office block where it remained. The shop floor waited and waited. Comments to the effect that it was only to be expected that the MD should have a pee and coffee break gave way to sarcastic comment about him not wanting to see 'the likes of us'. The shop floor was wrong. The MD did come to see them, at about 3.00 in the afternoon.

A party of about six men and one woman appeared in the workshops, led by the local manager. The MD, smoking a large cigar, received brief explanations of work and equipment as he passed by. None of the employees were spoken to although they did at times get close enough to receive a whiff of brandy fumes. The entourage remained silent until the party reached the last port of call. This was a toolmakers' workshop which had racks of tools on the walls. One of a set of spanners was missing.

'Oh,' exclaimed the woman in the party, 'you seem to have lost one of your spanners.' The chief toolmaker, to whom this pointless remark was made, said nothing – at the time. A few minutes in the toolmakers' room brought the visit to an end and the party departed at about 4.00 pm. The total length of the visit was about six hours, of which one hour was spent touring the workshops.

The comments of the workforce cannot be printed verbatim here, and some of them would take up too much space. The general reaction can be summarised as follows:

1 The MD spent most of the time eating and drinking.
2 None of the party spoke to anyone except (quote) 'that overdressed cow' who pointed out the missing spanner.
3 Cigars and brandy fumes might have been acceptable if any interest had been shown in the work being done.

4 The employees and their work were of no importance and
   all the preparations for the visit were a 'bloody joke'.
Note: It has been said that a famous (now retired) politician
always waited until the TV cameras were gone before he lit
up a fat cigar. Otherwise he smoked a proletarian pipe!

Morale in the factory dropped sharply when, for the sake of a
few words here and there, some interested questions and the
odd congratulatory remark, a visiting VIP could have done
wonders. It is no accident that many Japanese VIPs dress in
overalls and spend a lot of time with, and are visible to, the
workforce.

An account of another state visit can be given verbatim.
This concerned a branch shop in a large national chain. The
visitor was a director, not a CE, but the difference in status
meant little to the staff at the shop who regarded all above
local manager as on a par with the heavenly host. This is
what a junior staff member said:

> We prepared for the visit by lots of extra attention to filling
> the shelves, cleaning etc. We were all keyed up and
> excited about it. We did not know when they would arrive
> which meant we were on tenterhooks all morning.
>
> When they did arrive, they paused inside the front
> doors for the director to comb his hair. They walked
> through the shop peering at things and pointing and ges-
> ticulating. They spoke to only the manager and two heads
> of department, mostly in a corner of the shop. They then
> strolled off and were served tea in the manager's office.
>
> They did not speak to any shop floor staff.
>
> Most of the staff were very disappointed and felt they
> should at least have spoken to one sales assistant in each
> department. After all, they are the backbone of the shop.
>
> The following day we received the message that the
> shop looked very nice and thanks for the hard work. This
> was passed on by the assistant manager. It would have
> been nice if the director could have said it to us himself.

It is difficult to imagine what the visiting VIP hopes to gain by ignoring the people he is visiting. Some individuals may feel that they are too important to talk to the 'ordinary' staff or that by doing so they are somehow reducing their status. Such VIPs should take a lesson from no less a person than the Queen of England. She and all her family make a point of talking to all and sundry. This has not yet resulted in any visible loss of respect or status – rather the reverse.

It seems a good idea to conclude this topic by mentioning an example of a really *good* state visit, a day at a branch office. During the day the CE avoided drifting aimlessly from one department to another with a large entourage. He went alone and not only spoke *with* (not to) everyone in each department but also asked them detailed and intelligent questions about their work. This took up more time than originally allowed and, with apologies to those staff not seen, he promised to return for another session. This promise was kept and within a month he was back for a second attempt.

Before anyone suggests that he was obviously a man with plenty of spare time, it can be firmly stated that this CE was very busy indeed. But in his opinion his visits were a vital part of his job and were given priority over other, important, demands on his time.

What then are the benefits of this approach? Firstly, the CE gained a lot of knowledge of what went on in the company for which he was responsible. Secondly, he gained the respect and admiration of staff, who knew that he was a very busy man. 'It's so nice that he should take such obvious interest in us,' said one employee. Thirdly, he raised the morale of the staff and improved their interest in the work they had to do. Obviously if the 'big man' thinks the work is worthy of detailed discussion, then it must be important. Anyone who feels that his work is important, and his efforts appreciated, will devote more care and energy to it. That in turn contributes to profits, which are a prime responsibility of every chief executive.

32

Action checklist (especially for chief executives)

1 Avoid interfering. Monitor and observe what is going on in the company but do delegate.

2 If your role is not clear to you, obtain independent advice. A professional study and evaluation of the role of the board as a whole may be valuable, e.g. in exposing lack of clarity in objectives or responsibilities.

3 Avoid concentrating on (or favouring) the parts of the business you are most familiar with. The chief is responsible for *the whole* business. Ensure that you have a good working knowledge of all parts of the business and constant communication with all parts.

4 Beware of the 'good life'. Keep business meals and drink to an absolute minimum. This will also provide more time to communicate with the heads of departments and all the other vital activities.

5 Avoid sudden and unnecessary 'flushes of enthusiasm'. These can cost money. Maintain a steady interest in everything going on in the business.

6 Avoid favouritism.

7 Compare your style with that described on pages 26 and 27.

8 Use state visits profitably. Plan them carefully, including in your plan the following points:
   (a) The objective behind the visit.
   (b) Routing and timing to have the best effect.
   (c) Briefing (before the visit) on who's who.
   (d) Ideas, thoughts and attitudes to be 'put over' during the visit.
   (e) Information to be gained – including attitudes of individuals.
   (f) A means for obtaining 'feedback' after the visit to aid evaluation of its usefulness.

3

THE MANAGER AND THE ACCOUNTANTS

There is nothing essentially wrong with accountants. Some of us have good friends who are accountants, some of us have allowed our children to marry accountants – but heaven preserve the company which abdicates its management role and allows the accountants to take over!

One of the most puzzling aspects of company management is the willingness, even eagerness, to regard all financial matters as the exclusive preserve of the accountant. Even sole proprietors of small businesses will allow accountants to dominate their activities. This is not only unnecessary but unwise.

There may be a number of reasons for this abdication, varying from case to case, but one reason always seems to be present – the managers have not taken the trouble to learn some very simple accounting techniques. They are therefore forced into a position where the accountants have a unique knowledge, which enables them, with a suitable display of mystical terms, to assume control.

'Management tools' such as budgeting, cash flow forecasting, project evaluation and break-even point calculation should be second nature to any manager worthy of the name. This will allow the manager to manage and the accountant to get on with his real job – bookkeeping, providing management with 'how we are doing' information and giving advice.

It is important for managers, especially the more senior

ones, to distinguish between bookkeeping and management. The former consists of keeping the records of cash in and cash out, collections and payments (within rules laid down by management) and preparing the statutory annual returns. But deciding when to launch a new product, whether or not to make an investment or what level of stock to hold is a manager's job. The accountant can help but he should not control. Unfortunately, it seems that whenever the accountant does gain control, all entrepreneurial flair disappears. Not only will the accountant swamp management in figures but he will hedge them around with all kinds of caveats and mumbo-jumbo.

This statement will cause the accountants to howl with protest! 'It is not mumbo-jumbo,' they will say. 'It is vital financial analysis.' That would be fine if it were always true, but it is not. The proof is the endless bickering in the accounting professional bodies as to whether or not their techniques are valid.

The year 1982, in the Institute of Chartered Accountants, was marked by a top level wrangle over Inflation Accounting, a particular piece of mumbo-jumbo launched on the unsuspecting business world in 1977 under the name of Current Cost Accounting. (Accountants seem to derive great satisfaction from inventing two or more names for the same thing.)

This accounting method was supposed to take care of the problem of financial reporting in an era of high inflation. By 1982 the Institute's 73,000 members were being asked to vote on the abandonment of the inflation accounting rules. The subject was still being debated several years later!

In the meantime a system designed to cover *every* imaginable kind of business seems to have confused not only boards of directors but accountants as well. The fact is that a shareholder presented with a report showing a 20 per cent increase in profits needs only to know to what extent inflation has contributed. If the contribution covered half of the increase, then he knows that his company performed about 10 per cent better. That is simple enough and requires no confusing (and expensive) jiggering with the books.

Some accountants have insisted that current cost accounting is necessary for tax purposes. That would be so if tax on company profits was calculated *after* adjustments for inflation, but this is not the case.

Another example of mumbo-jumbo is DCF (discounted cash flow). Whatever happened to that? At one time it was the alleged answer to every manager's prayer when evaluating an investment. It now seems to have faded away.

During a course on finance at the business studies department of the Polytechnic of Central London an elderly accountant gave a series of ways in which an investment project could be evaluated (including using DCF). At the end he said that there was one other method, often as good as the rest. He then wrote one word on the blackboard – 'HUNCH'. Allowing for the, perhaps unusual, fact that this was an accountant with a sense of humour, this was a serious warning not to allow complex mathematics of the pounds and pence to take over.

There are other ways in which the accountant can confuse the manager. Perhaps some of the following ring a bell or two.

Book value

Accountants love to have 'book values', i.e. purely notional, arbitrary figures in the books purporting to be the values of assets. The figures are arrived at by taking the original cost of an item purchased and reducing its value by a certain amount each year until it is 'written down' to zero. This process has some value in determining annual book profits but no value in real life.

The fact is that money is spent at the time of purchase and not in instalments over a number of years (unless the purchase is made by some form of leasing system). The problem is that the accountant places a seemingly magical value on the book value of the asset. This becomes apparent if it should be decided to sell the item. The accountant trots out the book value and seems to think that this will decide the selling price. It will not. The selling price is the amount someone else will pay for the item, and since the buyer will not be in the least impressed by the seller's book value, the latter is irrelevant.

Accountants have been known to fight against a sale at a price below book value as if keeping the item gathering dust in a store is better than getting some money for it. They have also been known to suggest the book value as the price to be charged when it was obvious that the market would pay more.

A possible illustration of this situation is the one-year-old Rolls-Royce or Range Rover. Such cars are probably worth more than the new car list price. Presumably the accountant would be satisfied with the list price from which he has deducted 20 per cent depreciation.

More than one manager has lost money by taking notice of the accountant's book value. It is likely that if these managers understood what book value really meant, they would have acted differently.

A further proof of the absurdity in book values is the divergence of views held, and acted on, by accountants when deciding the rate of depreciation. The accountant will take a view on the useful life of an item and use the number of years decided on as a depreciation period. Thus, if he decides that a filing cabinet has a life of five years, he may well depreciate at the rate of 20 per cent of the purchase price per annum.

Accountants seem unable to answer the following questions satisfactorily:

1 Why choose five years? Why not three or four or six – or even ten? There have been cases where, in the *same* company, *different* periods of years for identical items were chosen. (By the way, the number of years chosen is not always explained by tax considerations. The Inland Revenue has its own ideas about depreciation periods.)

THE MANAGER AND THE ACCOUNTANTS

2 Why depreciate at a regular, i.e. equal, amount per annum? The real value of most capital equipment drops very sharply in the first year compared with the rest. If the depreciated value is meant to represent the realisable asset value, then surely depreciation should reflect this. The problem is that accountants vary in their views as to what the book value really *does* represent.

3 Where is the logic when an item has been written down on the books to nil, when it clearly still has a value?

4 Where is the logic when an item is faithfully written down each year when its value is in fact increasing? A rare case no doubt, but where are the accountant's rules to cover this situation?

Finally, as a manager don't allow yourself to believe that depreciation is a means to save up money to buy a replacement. It isn't and it doesn't! You will still have to fork out the *cash* from income, reserves, or borrowings – whatever the accountant has done with his books.

To buy or not to buy

Another situation which arises from time to time concerns the problem of what to do when you have just spent a lot of money on, say, a machine, and then been offered a better one. Suppose, for example, the manager has very recently spent £1,000 on a Productowhizz machine with a running cost (including labour) of £100 a week. Along comes another smart young salesman offering the latest in technology – the Electrowhizz for £1,100. The running cost of this machine is only £50 per week.

What should the manager do?

Accountants are likely to say: 'We have just spent £1,000 on the Productowhizz, and it will not be written off for four years. We do not need both machines and the Productowhizz standing idle would be a shocking waste.' This is emotional thinking and quite wrong.

The manager must ignore the 'book value' red herring and swallow his sadness at having just spent £1,000, which, if he had waited only a few weeks, could have been used to buy a better machine. Secondly, he must forget any past expenditure – even in the very recent past. The money has gone and cannot be recovered. Remember, writing down the value each year on the books does *not* bring the money back! Thirdly he must consider only the aspects now relevant, i.e. (a) future costs, and (b) avoidable costs. The future cost is £1,100 for an Electrowhizz and the avoidable cost is the difference in running costs. He will save £50 a week by investing in the new machine and he will 'get his money back' in only twenty-two weeks. From then on he is £50 a week better off.

The accountant faced with this argument is inclined to drag in further mumbo-jumbo about 'opportunity costs'. By this he is implying that the £1,100 could be better spent elsewhere. This may be true, but the manager should check it out first. (Of course it may be possible to improve the position by selling the unwanted Productowhizz to someone who has not heard of its more efficient rival.)

The *facts* and the opportunity should be explained by the accountant, and the manager must insist that this is done. Don't give up after the first barrage of bookkeepers' jargon – or the second barrage either!

There was a classic example of the application of emotional mumbo-jumbo at national level in the early 1970s when Concorde was being completed. Estimates of development costs were repeatedly being revised (upwards) and the politicians were making the customary noises. There came a final stage when £40,000,000 more was requested. The politicians were incensed and there were righteous cries of 'Abandon the project; we have spent enough already'.

The politicians were misled and misleading. Having spent the money, it could not be recovered by abandoning the project. Therefore, the only *relevant* question to be answered at this final stage was 'Are we willing to pay £40,000,000 for a supersonic airliner?'

Action checklist

1 Learn the basics of accounting – they are not all that complicated. (See Appendix 1 for suggestions on painless ways to learn.)

2 Obtain your accountant's advice – then make an informed decision yourself.

3 In particular beware of 'book values' and other smokescreens. If your accountant trots out some jargon you do not understand, insist that he translates it for you. All jargon terms can be put into normal language if we really try.

4

THE MANAGER AND CONFLICT

It seems that members of the human race are unable to live with each other without conflict. The periods when, for example, European nations have all been at peace with each other or outsiders are shorter in total than the periods of war.

This tendency to conflict is an ever-present danger in business and is yet another problem for the manager. Part of the manager's job is to be aware of conflict and do something about it. Many managers seem to prefer the easier option of turning a blind eye to the battles going on around them. One senior man was actually pleased to have conflict between his departments on the basis that (a) it was easier to rule a divided team and (b) when fighting each other, they had no time to gang up on him!

Observations suggest that in reality all parties gain more by co-operation than by conflict. This particularly applies to the manager. Let's examine some of the causes of conflict that can be found.

Overlapping jobs

It is obvious that if two individuals are given overlapping responsibilities (i.e. badly designed or missing job descriptions), a row, sometime, is virtually inevitable. The row might occur, for example, when something important is neglected because both assumed that the other was handling the problem. At the inquest they will blame each other. The manager's role is equally obvious – to see that areas of authority and responsibility are clear and distinct.

It is harder to spot the problem where departmental responsibilities overlap. Part of the difficulty is that departments, even more than individuals, will assume responsibilities to gain status, professional standing or to meet group ambition. This can be hard to identify because a number of people are involved and the group feeling is often unspoken.

A new manager once took over the management of an organisation and methods department which was in constant conflict with the computer department. The conflict was caused by the following *similarities* between the departments:

(a) Similar technical skills existed in both departments.
(b) Both departments were expected to find opportunities for improvements to systems.
(c) Both departments had to deal with the same outside suppliers, who provided both general office equipment *and* computer equipment.
(d) Both departments were under pressure to prove their worth.

Running battles were going on over who should develop a new idea. Men from the O & M department felt aggrieved if one of their ideas was 'taken over' by the computer boys on the basis that there was an aspect of computing in it. The computer boys were aggrieved when the reverse situation applied and also when an O & M man talked to the suppliers, who were not averse to trying to sell the company a computer system via the O & M department. This caused much gnashing of teeth in the computer manager's office.

All in all, things were bad. There was little or no trust or co-operation and the atmosphere was unpleasant to work in. The O & M manager's predecessor had taken up the problem with the more senior manager responsible for both departments but the big boss was unable or unwilling to act.

The O & M manager therefore approached the computer manager and put his cards on the table.

His argument was as follows:

(a) We all have to work here, so let's make it as pleasant as possible.
(b) Senior management will not clarify our departmental roles and it is this lack of clarity (definition) which is at the root of the conflicts.
(c) We have enough brains between us to define our roles to our mutual satisfaction, so let's do it.

The computer manager, who was just as fed up with the bickering as his colleague was, readily agreed, and between them they laid down some ground rules. From that day things improved out of all recognition, and not only was everyone happier when trust was established but more and better quality work was produced. Ultimately many projects were carried out by teams made up of members from both departments – which, in systems work, is how it should be.

The lesson to be stated is that if a manager's boss won't act, then the manager must do it himself. The frustrating thing is that the boss (who is paid more anyway) will probably get the kudos from the action of his subordinates – action he was not willing to take himself. 'T'was ever thus!', as the man said.

There is some interesting comment on this problem in a book by C. B. Handy (*Understanding Organisations*, Penguin 1976). Handy reports that when a group of managers were asked for their thoughts on conflict, 87 per cent felt that it was rarely coped with and attempts to do so were inadequate, and 65 per cent thought that the *most important* unsolved problem was that top management appeared unable to help them overcome rivalries between groups.

Lack of understanding of other people's jobs

This is a commonplace problem and is easily solved by bringing the people together. For example, a consultant was asked by a 'head office' department to examine the work of a 'country office' department. The former maintained that the latter was slow in processing work and not very intelligent. It was alleged that it referred back transactions which were perfectly straightforward, and this proved how dim its staff all were.

The country office in turn alleged that the 'other lot' lacked intelligence – demonstrated by the large number of errors in the work sent in by them. These errors, it was stated, caused the delays and most of them *had* to be referred back.

Analysis showed that about 30 per cent of all the documents sent to the country office department had errors of omission or commission. Further investigations showed that most of the errors (and *all* those of omission) were caused by a lack of understanding of what the country office had to do.

The problem was eventually solved when both sides met and discussed the job to be done. Hitherto all contact had been by vitriolic memorandum or abusive 'phone call. Some redesign of the forms helped matters but above all in importance were the face-to-face discussions at which the amazing discovery was made that the 'other lot' were not such bad people after all.

A similar problem, but this time to do with departments in a number of European countries, was solved in the same way.

Departments in England, Holland, France, Germany, Belgium, Italy and the Scandinavian countries had to send each other documents and information concerning shipments of product. Each national department was utterly convinced that the others were a worthless rabble who failed to understand the simplest matters. Product code numbers were 'always' wrong when another country wrote them. Customer addresses were 'always' wrong. Special instructions were 'always' ignored, and so on.

There were, it was found, a number of weaknesses in the system and such things as lists of code numbers out of date in some places. These system weaknesses no doubt caused a number of genuine operating faults but, in addition, the degree of emnity between the departments (supported in some cases by national prejudice) was such that people looked for trouble – and had become expert at finding it.

A meeting of all the heads of departments was arranged in London to thrash out the problems. After a frosty start (accusations thrown around required some firm chairmanship) much progress was made in clearing up misunderstandings. The 'reason why' was repeatedly explained and the light of understanding of each other's problems began to dawn. Gradually two discoveries were made:

(a) The problems were in the main simple ones – but with large consequences.
(b) The 'other lot' were quite decent people after all.

The latter feeling was reinforced by a good dinner, plenty to drink and a noisy evening in a nightclub.

People who previously really disliked each other, but had never met, now saw that their colleagues were much like themselves. They too had a job to do, customers to satisfy, staff problems, warehouse space problems and so on. The other person was also a human being (contrary to previous belief) who enjoyed a joke, a drink or two and was also having problems with teenage kids. This initial get-together was repeated every six months and valuable work was done in not merely clearing up problems but in generating new ideas for the future.

Lack of discipline

A small sales force complete with company cars and expense accounts required the back-up service of a team of office clerks. The salesmen, whose status, above that of the clerks, was strengthened by possession of the cars and expense accounts, regarded the work of the clerks as beneath them. They extended this to an abhorrence of form filling, even to the point where sales order forms and customers' instructions were being neglected.

This is a common problem. A few minutes talk with anyone servicing a sales force will reveal all or some of the following views, which were forcefully expressed by the sales office clerks:

(a) They don't fully fill in the order form and we have to ring the customers to get the facts. This annoys the customers and delays order processing.
(b) They leave out special requirements such as 'no deliveries on Mondays' and we get the blame when it happens.
(c) They just go round drinking gin with the customers and we do all the real work.

The ingredients of conflict are contained in these feelings. Further ingredients were found in the salesmen's viewpoint:

(a) We send in the orders promptly but that idle lot in the office don't process them promptly.
(b) If that lot in the office can find a way to mess up a delivery, they will do it.

The two sides were at loggerheads for no other reason than one side (or both) lacked the discipline to carry out their work with sufficient attention to detail.

Much the same antagonism can be found between insurance salesmen and insurance technicians, between insurance brokers and office technicians and between order entry clerks and warehouse staff. The solution lies in having a good, well designed procedure which everyone follows to the letter, combined with a knowledge of each other's jobs and the reason why things must be done in the prescribed fashion.

The 'my department' attitude

A departmental manager was hotly defending the actions of

a man reporting to him. He made references to 'my staff' and 'my department'. His boss, listening to his diatribe, suddenly interrupted and said: 'The problem we are dealing with is caused by your attitude. You refer to *your* department and *your* staff. They are not *yours*, they are part of the company.'

At first the manager did not see the point of this remark, but after some thought he realised what his boss was getting at. He also realised that a lot of problems can arise from this possessive attitude, which inhibits self-examination and self-criticism and encourages a 'defend our actions at all costs' posture. This can cause conflict between two managers holding the same 'my department' attitude.

Leadership is needed to prevent these situations arising. They are not all obvious and not all at a major level. Energy is consumed in umpteen petty squabbles, ranging from who sits next to the radiator to which section is first on the tea lady's rounds. This last example is no exaggeration, it really did happen! The subject was twice on the agenda of a departmental managers' meeting and still not resolved more than a year later!

Finally, watch out for a trap into which we can all fall. A manager can develop the belief that a colleague is out to 'fix him' or otherwise behave like a rat. The feeling builds up until, at a routine meeting, say, the suspicious manager launches an attack on his colleague. Lo and behold, the colleague returns the fire, thus confirming the manager's suspicion that the beggar *was* out to damage him all the time. With suspicions now being proved correct on one side and a fiercely defensive posture assumed on the other, both parties can now enter into a number of years of mutual hatred with all the damage that entails.

Sexist attitudes

Conflict can also be caused by prejudice based on sexism – most commonly men being prejudiced against women. This is now less marked than in previous years, when, as in the case of gentlemen's clubs, women were positively barred from certain boardrooms. However, the problem is still with us and conflict between the sexes goes on. This conflict does not necessarily restrict itself to the main antagonists but can spill over, as is illustrated by the case of Rosalind.

She was a well qualified accountant with a somewhat shy disposition. She worked for a company with a distinct 'male flavour' where the opinions of women on business matters were often treated with amused condescension. However, one of Rosalind's male colleagues had a high opinion of her abilities and arranged for her to take part in an important new product development scheme – to the irritation of the (male) chief accountant, who clearly thought that a male accountant should do the job.

Rosalind worked hard on the financial aspects of the scheme and produced some first-class forecasts and plans. These were too good for the chief accountant to accept and he made a point of severely criticising each and every idea that Rosalind put forward at meetings of the project team. Not only did this depress Rosalind (who was too shy to fight back) but it annoyed other members of the team, who were impressed with Rosalind's work.

The outcome was a series of disagreements between the chief accountant and the rest of the team and, sadly, Rosalind's resignation. The (male) replacement for Rosalind was not so imaginative and, unlike Rosalind, did not get on well with the team. Eventually the scheme was scrapped in an atmosphere of disagreement over the likely financial outcome. (By the way, Rosalind is now a successful director of a flourishing company.)

Resolving the problem of conflict brought about by sexist attitudes is far from easy in view of the well entrenched attitudes in many companies. One successful female executive who feels that she has the problem 'under control', if not beaten, offers the following advice:

It is impossible to avoid conflict completely, particularly

with the man who believes that 'the woman's place is in the home, tied to the kitchen sink' and does not mind letting everyone know it. In this situation the woman must stand up for herself, otherwise she loses respect. However, she might remember the following:

- Keep cool – never lose your temper and never resort to tears.
- Be yourself – business is not the place for feminine wiles, but men still like the women around them to look and act like women. Remember sexism works both ways and men can feel threatened by the woman who tries to be one of the boys.
- Ignore small irritations – some men call all women 'dear' and do not mean to be insulting. Turn it into a joke, call them 'dear' back.
- Treat all your colleagues the same, male and female.
- Stand up for yourself – do not allow yourself to be appointed minute taker or coffee fetcher at every meeting. Make sure that everyone takes a turn.

Finally, remember that being a woman can be an advantage. Most men will at least hear your argument without interruption – a courtesy seldom extended to their male colleagues. Use this advantage to the full. Present your case logically, succinctly and in a well thought out manner and it's much harder for anyone to shoot your argument down – especially if he is only doing so because you are female.

Clearly it is the manager's responsibility to watch out for and deal with conflict based on sexist attitudes. It must be made clear to all that prejudice of this type is not only indefensible but is damaging and will not be tolerated. Above all the manager must avoid any personal sexist behaviour.

In the next chapter some of the less obvious but equally damaging forms of prejudice are examined.

Action checklist

1 If conflict exists, do something about it. Festering wounds do not heal themselves by magic.

2 Determine the causes of conflict and remove them.

3 Make sure that people get together, and understand each other and the demands of their jobs.

4 Avoid defending 'my department' at all costs. Be prepared to be objective and self-critical.

5 Examine your attitudes to the opposite sex. Be sure that your actions are prompted by an objective study of the facts – not by an 'instinctive' refusal to agree with someone because of his or her sex. Treat all your colleagues as equals and as fairly as is humanly possible, regardless of gender.

5

THE MANAGER AND PREJUDICE

It seems that all human beings are prone to prejudice, and if one accepts that all managers are human beings, then all managers are prone to prejudice. This is demonstrated time and time again and frequently in a most damaging way. But, managers have a responsibility to form judgements on the basis of objective thinking and facts – if only to avoid injustice. Prejudice has no place in professional management.

The moralities of prejudice are not the only considerations for the manager. The business, and the manager himself, can be harmed by it.

A very bright young man (mid-twenties), with a short but impressive track record, was being interviewed for a job. He gave good, clear answers to the questions put to him and gradually gave the impression that he would be a good prospect. His references were good and he seemed to have a balanced and pleasant personality.

When the young man left the room, the senior man present said, to the surprise of his two colleagues, 'Well, we certainly don't want him!' This statement was made very firmly in a tone which implied that the man was either a crook or was suffering from an unmentionable and very catching disease. The senior man then gave his assessment of the candidate, which went something like this: 'I judge a man from his appearance. The candidate showed – from his long hair – that he is a feckless type, unreliable and probably lazy. The sort of chap who hangs about in discos and not the sort we want here.'

This was in 1971 when the 'short back and sides' was beginning to go out of fashion. Our unfortunate candidate had allowed his hair to touch his collar, as had many existing, and satisfactory employees of the company. He did not get the job, which was probably just as well for him, because nine years later he was marketing director of a substantial company and was very successful. (It is interesting to note that the firm critic of 'long hair' had retained his own short back and sides and retained it throughout the year when all his male colleagues had fallen in with the long hair fashion.)

This principle of not liking people who are different from ourselves is mirrored in a tendency to favour those who are similar to ourselves. A cartoon in a business magazine showed a personnel manager interviewing a man for a job. The two men were identical in appearance. The personnel manager was saying, 'I like the look of you, young man.' There was a great deal of truth in that cartoon.

Similarity preferences are not limited to appearances. Most people also feel that others with similar work backgrounds must be superior – if only because we believe in ourselves and our own qualities. Engineers will favour other engineers and ex-service people look for others with a military background. The following are real life preferences expressed by managers and mostly based on similar experiences or background:

Ex-servicemen
Public schoolboys
Red Brick graduates
Oxbridge graduates
Thin people
Northern accents
Southern accents
People who walk quickly(!)

Conversely, real life *dislikes* of people with any of these same attributes have been noted, including the otherwise very intelligent manager who said 'I don't like Old Etonians'. Presumably he disliked every single one of them.

There was also the manager who declared that he would never employ anyone who had been to Sussex University. The reason he gave was that a graduate of Sussex had turned up for an interview in an old army battledress. This was enough to condemn all Sussex men, even the ones who could be of great value to the manager and his Company.

At about this stage all readers should be agreeing that prejudice exists but assuring themselves that they are not guilty of it. The truth of this can be tested by an entertaining 'party game' which can be tried out on colleagues – all of whom are, like ourselves, too intelligent to be prejudiced.

Divide your colleagues into two groups and, separately, show each group a photograph of an 'ordinary' looking man wearing unremarkable clothing and a 'neutral' expression. Casually tell one group that the man is a NUPE shop steward and the other group that he is a bank manager. Then ask each group to describe the man's character from what the photograph shows of him.

The answers are likely to be very revealing of the built-in attitudes of the group and its individual members towards shop stewards and bank managers. The people expressing their views will of course say that their conclusions are based on the man's shifty expression/honest face/belligerent posture/relaxed manner, etc.

Other combinations can be tried. For example,

An auditor	v	a betting shop manager
A tax inspector	v	a publican
A theology lecturer	v	an insurance salesman
A racing car driver	v	a bus driver
An SAS captain	v	a ledger clerk

The results will illustrate one danger that a manager must guard against: the natural propensity to base judgements, and make decisions, on preconditioning and stereotyping.

Managers must also be on guard against the assessment of the whole person on the basis of one characteristic, such as long hair meaning fecklessness, laziness and unreliability. Another real-life example concerned the very able research chemist who solemnly and seriously stated that people who wear bow ties have unstable personalities.

From observations of managers' attitudes to colleagues and subordinates – and the results of those attitudes – it can be shown that prejudice can be made to 'prove itself correct'. If, for example, a manager favours a young new employee because of, say, his social background, it is likely that the young employee will succeed: not, as the boss supposes, because he is the 'right type' but because the boss, believing him to be the right type, gives him more support and opportunity.

The reverse can also be frequently observed. The employee who is, say, physically unattractive to the boss, seems to do badly. This can result simply because the boss is cool and unfriendly to such an employee and the coldness of manner demotivates.

A particular form of prejudice occurs after mergers and takeovers. In one such case, *four years* after the takeover, employees of the bought-out company were at a disadvantage. Smith Ltd, having taken over Brown Ltd, ended up with a mixture of Smith-men and Brown-men. One of the first questions asked when deciding on a man's future (or even before judging the quality of his work!) was 'Is he a Smith-man or a Brown-man?' or even 'Is he one of ours or one of theirs?' Time and again reports were played down, good and quantifiable results condemned and, at least once, a promotion denied because the employee concerned was 'one of theirs'. How stupid can a manager get?

Conversely this form of prejudice can be a great boon to the 'loyal', long-serving employee, who can be overrated because he is a company man. The word 'loyal' is placed in inverted commas because prejudice can distort this virtue. The man who never rocks the boat and always agrees with the VIPs is regarded as 'loyal'. In reality he probably has never had an original idea in his life, and, if he has, lacks the courage to express it. On the other hand, the creative, imaginative man who suggests radical new approaches can be condemned as 'disloyal', though he is a valuable employee.

This brand of prejudice permits new ideas from the company men but not from the others. The Brown-man is likely to have every suggestion treated at best as silly and at worst as deliberate sabotage.

So, take care. The next time you receive a suggestion or interview a man for a job try to be objective. Try not to launch straight into opposition just because the person concerned is a bearded Old Etonian with a bow-tie. He may be the best man for miles around.

Action checklist

1 Identify and admit your prejudices.

2 Suppress your prejudices as far as you can. At least evaluate them and try to be balanced and reasonable.

3 Be prepared for prejudice in others and allow for it.

BIRCH

6

THE WORKAHOLIC MANAGER

Fred, an up-and-coming executive, was gripped by the fascination of his job and had become a workaholic. For years he bored his friends with his obsession with work, became a 'Saturday morning father' to his children and was a pain in the backside to his colleagues. Fortunately he was cured before he became a manager and thus avoided some of the worst effects – including a heart attack. The cure was brought about, quite unwittingly, by a German colleague, who managed a large department of the company in Dusseldorf.

Fred visited him on business many times over a period of about three years and was always impressed by the efficiency of his operation and the attitude of his staff. His department was always a pleasure to visit, since everyone in it was, it seemed, always cheerful and smiling. Fred also had many opportunities to confirm the high standard of efficiency in the department, high productivity and a consistent quality in the work done.

He was struck by the fact that whenever he visited this manager, even at short notice, he always had time for discussions and never seemed to be in a hurry. It was obvious that he worked hard and that he carried a good deal of responsibility. Despite this he always had time for strategic discussions, for planning ahead or to debate ways and means to improve the company's operations.

Fred studied the methods of his German colleague and

noted the four main characteristics of his approach:

1 Careful selection of staff.
2 Planned and effective training of staff.
3 Delegation.
4 Constant communication to and from his staff in a relaxed
   and friendly atmosphere.

One day, out of the blue, a 'crisis' arose in the Swedish part
of the company and Fred dashed off to Stockholm to help. It
was easy for him to dash off like this, because of his 'staff'
position, with no line management responsibilities to tie
him down.

Fred realised, after spending a couple of days in
Stockholm, that his German colleague would be the ideal
man to help with some of the technical problems. His knowledge of certain technical aspects was much greater. Fred
telephoned him and, with some trepidation, asked him if he
could spare the time to visit Stockholm and help sort things
out. He agreed immediately, joined Fred the next day and
stayed for four days.

At the end of the four days, Fred was in the course of
thanking him for his help when he asked how it was that a
manager with considerable responsibilities could 'drop
everything' and spend a number of days away from his base.
Fred took careful note of his reply, which was roughly as
follows: 'Fred, a good manager is a lazy man. If he is lazy he
delegates everything. That way I get more time to drink beer
and see the lovely girls in the Stockholm office'. This attitude
is the exact opposite of that of the workaholic and it made
Fred realise that he was going the wrong way. He was not
likely to be a success if he became a manager. From that time
he changed course and tried to be lazy.

What then, is a workaholic? Based on close observation of
three workaholics, the symptoms are as follows:

1 The workaholic can be of any age and at any level in management. He comes in early each day, works through his
   lunch period (a sandwich at the desk or a working lunch

with colleagues) and goes home late. He will work on the train (if senior enough to have a chauffeur-driven car he will work in the car) and work at home in the evening.

2 He will work during weekends and skips his holidays.

3 He is usually a happy man, immersed in his obsession with his job. He is, however, impatient at lunch and similar social meetings with people who want to discuss the cricket results, politics or whatever. He will maintain a polite interest for the sake of appearances but cannot wait to steer the subject back to business.

4 He often has a history of 'mobility' to suit his job. One of the three subjects had moved house eleven times in fourteen years to further his career. (What his wife and children felt about this is easy to imagine!)

5 He is likely to be personally efficient in the sense that his own output is of high quality, with every detail carefully checked and rechecked.

Despite this last attribute, he is a menace to his firm and his colleagues. He is also a danger to himself in terms of his domestic happiness and personal health, but that is his private affair. If he wants to die young and alone, that is his privilege. His inadequacies as a manager are a different matter, and observations suggest that the workaholic can damage the business in the following ways.

Damage caused by workaholics

The creation of pseudo-workaholics

This character is an unfortunate subordinate, who would love to go home each day at a reasonable hour but feels that because his workaholic boss stays late in the office night after night, he must do the same. Sometimes he (the pseudo-workaholic) spends his time actually working, thus giving a wrong impression of the work capacity of the department. This prevents more staff being taken on and eventually means that the pseudos are stuck with the long hours for ever.

Sometimes the pseudo merely pretends to work. One such unfortunate could be seen sitting with papers in front of him, staring into space, for an hour or two after normal closing time. Should the boss appear, he would rapidly assume an alert appearance and seem to be concentrating hard on a thorny problem. Having kept up the pretence of work for an appropriate period, the pseudo will leave the office accompanied by sufficient noise (coughing, door banging, etc.) to make sure the boss knows when he is leaving, i.e. late. He will carry a briefcase to give the impression of taking work home. He will turn up late, and breathless, to meetings – thus wasting other people's time. He apologises for being late and explains that he is 'desperately busy' and was caught up in an inescapable and urgent matter just as he was about to leave for the meeting.

All of this is to give an impression of the dedication which the boss himself displays. The impression can become a reality if, as sometimes happens, the pseudo eventually becomes a real workaholic with a real addiction.

The whole thing is not only inhuman (why on earth should someone have such guilt feeling thrust upon him that he will *pretend* to work and give up his private life to do it!) but is also prone to Parkinsonism. The workaholic manager is not a delegator, and his staff, to find something to do in the extra hours, will create work. They will also spin out work during the normal day to have something to do in the evening. This gives a false impression of work capacity, slows down essential tasks and diverts costly resources to 'created work'.

Reduction of morale
Lack of delegation means that the staff *know* they are spinning out trivial matters and this is not a means to obtain satisfaction from work. Resentment at having to maintain the pretence simmers away, damaging the individual and reducing loyalty to the company.

Waste of resources
The workaholic is wasting human resources, if not damaging

them. Observation suggests that his obsession with detail, and taking a lot of time over it, allows him too little time to spend on planning and communication and organising his workforce.

A fascinating fact arising from observation is that the workaholic is normally ill informed about what his staff are doing. He does not communicate with them to find out (or for any other reason) and this is why they can successfully pretend to be working. The manager should know what workloads really are and know that continual excessive overtime is suspect.

Creation of a long-term problem

There is one other problem which a workaholic creates – the aftermath of his departure. He normally leaves a mess behind, and the staff, mightily relieved at his departure, assume normal working hours. Output drops and demands are made for more staff. An increase in staff is resisted and it is difficult, without admitting what went on before, to justify the increase. The ensuing dissatisfaction can last for months.

Two workaholics were found by their staff to be intolerable – and bad managers. The first was 'too busy' to give any direction or support, and one of his staff went through a period of *nine months* without any discussion of his work at all! Fortunately, this employee was able to take the initiative and get on by himself. But he was deciding the priorities, not his boss!

The second was an 'early starter', who came into work about an hour early each day. His deputy made a habit of coming in ten to fifteen minutes early. The problem was that they had adjacent offices, and by the time the deputy came in, the boss was all keyed up to see him. Each day the boss discovered some wonderful new project (each more urgent and exciting than the last one). The early hours were obviously his 'creative time'.

The deputy would sneak past his door (always open), hoping he would not be seen. He was not a passionately early starter and was more effective if he could spend the first ten minutes or so gathering his thoughts over a cup of coffee. (This is particularly vital to many commuters, who need a little while to get over the ghastly and exhausting experiences of train and tube travel.) The boss almost always did see him and nearly every day called him in to explain his latest idea. The worst morning the deputy ever had was one on which he sat in the boss's office for about two hours listening to his excited explanations. He still had his coat on and was bursting for a pee when he finally emerged.

This boss retired early, broken in health (mental *and* physical) and it took his successor eighteen months to make the department truly efficient. Incurable workaholics would be best employed in setting up their own one-man businesses. They might end up millionaires, and even if they die an early death, they will at least have avoided making colleagues' lives a misery.

Action checklist

1 Decide if you are a workaholic. Tick each of the following if they apply to you:
   (a) I regularly work one or more hours voluntary unpaid overtime each day.
   (b) I prefer work to recreation.
   (c) I wait impatiently for Monday mornings.
   (d) I work on weekends.
   (e) I resent holidays but take them because my spouse insists.
   (f) I skip all or part of my holiday.
   (g) I have little or no time for family interests.
   (h) I am often irritated if I see my staff leaving work on time.
   (i) I find it difficult to keep a secretary – they seem to be unwilling to put in the effort I require.
   (j) I have no time for sports, hobbies or other recreation.
   (k) I have no time to delegate.
   If you tick two of the statements, regard it as a danger signal.
   Three to five ticks means you are 'over the edge'.
   Six or more ticks . . . .

2 If you are a workaholic, consider –
Are you efficient?
Is your department efficient?
Are your staff happy?
Do you have a good potential successor?
Do you want to remain a workaholic?

3 If the answer to any of the above questions is 'No' or 'Maybe', then take the following steps:
  (a) Review your own priorities. Are you over concerned with detail?
  (b) Give some of your time to your staff.
  (c) Remove unnecessary work from your department, delegate and slow down.
  (d) Put a stop to excessive hours worked as a matter of routine.
  (e) Work positively towards an economical and *managed* department.

7

THE MANAGER AND PROFIT

Members of the Socialist Workers Party can say that 'profit' is a dirty word. That is their privilege. The manager, who has a responsibility to his colleagues, staff and himself, must do his utmost to see that his company makes a profit. Bankrupt businesses do nothing to add to the joys of living but do contribute to the great army of unemployed.

Although every manager should find the necessity for profitable operations to be so obvious and so much in his own interest, both as an employee and a manager, it is surprising to find so many contrary attitudes. There are many managers who do not see themselves as being in any way responsible for profits. Such managers are most commonly found in 'support services' such as

Research and development
Accounting
Personnel
Public relations
Office administration

In other words, if the manager is not making the product or selling it, profit is regarded as someone else's headache.

This attitude is encouraged, if not caused, by the development of the notion of 'cost centres' as opposed to 'profit centres'. The latter is an organisational and operational concept which encourages positive action and a sense of responsibility, and is a 'mechanism' to improve results. The former can result in a passive approach to a department's role and an acceptance of expense without result as a justified position.

Take a look at a personnel department as an example. Personnel departments fall broadly into two categories – the record keepers and the academics.

Personnel departments

The record keepers
This type of personnel department occurs most frequently in small organisations (up to about 500 employees) and more particularly in family-dominated businesses. Their role is simple – to keep the personal records of employees (National Insurance No., home address, pension fund details, etc.). They might also do a little advertising for recruitment purposes and perhaps even interview candidates for very junior jobs.

The boss is either a former military man who did not make it beyond major or lieutenant-commander or a rather unimaginative woman who has been with the company since leaving school. The rest of the department comprises a typist (referred to by the boss as 'my secretary') and a downtrodden male clerk with worn-out collars and cuffs.

This unit carries out an entirely passive role. No ideas of any sort are asked for or offered. No contribution is made to management thinking and no action taken outside the bureaucracy laid down. This is not of course 'the fault' of the department, but how management wants things to be. This is how management sees its needs.

A consultant did get close to persuading one managing director that he should use his personnel department to provide him with information which would increase his ability to plan for profits. He rejected the idea because, as he said, 'There is no one in the department who is capable of any imaginative work.' Having created this situation himself, he preferred the easier option of using it as his excuse for not being able to act.

The department is thus seen, and set up, as an unavoidable if regrettable cost, to meet the statutory obligations of the firm. The cost will increase if the manager succeeds in obtaining more staff. This frequently happens because the manager can find so little satisfaction or status in the job that he strives to create a larger empire. Managers of these down-at-heel, dreary little departments seem to be particularly good at wingeing on about overwork and the need for more people.

The academics
At the other end of the size scale (huge organisations and, particularly, nationalised industries) one finds a very different but proportionately equally expensive cost centre. In this situation there is a Personnel Director of graduate status but probably not a business school graduate. He has reporting to him a range of departmental managers (all graduates but with no line management experience) heading up –

Industrial relations
Employee welfare and safety
Training and development
Salary and wage administration
Statistics and records   and so on, and so on . . .

All these functions will be maintained at group level and be duplicated at regional or divisional offices throughout the country.

To complete the picture there is the plush central office at a good address in the West End of London or downtown Manhattan. This office will be thickly carpeted and littered with status symbols such as the director's silver tea service. There will be an ample supply of under-utilised interview rooms and conference rooms, all costing dearly in rent and rates. Naturally, everyone has a secretary.

So here we have the department. It is of course a centre of costs. Huge costs! One such department was studied in detail by a systems analyst who calculated that if only essential or useful work was carried out the department could be reduced from 180 people to forty. Knowing that such a reduction would be politically unacceptable, he fudged his recommendations to suggest a 'more palatable' figure. In fact, nothing happened, as he was dealing with a nationalised industry.

What then do such departments do? They often work very hard and undertake masses of research work. This is all very fine but, and here is the rub, the results of the work are rarely, if ever, applied in the organisation.

The main characteristic of such departments is to write reports to themselves. Management in general is not interested and in any case rarely understands the reports produced. Among the reports one might find subjects such as the following:

'Social trends and their impact on manpower utilisation'
'Manpower projections in an environment of international uncertainty'
'Expectations of overtime and other premia in periods of high inflation'

It is possible to find numerous reports of this nature, which, apart from giving great pleasure to the authors, have never resulted in anything.

Top management also tends to ignore the sometimes complicated statistics produced by the larger personnel departments. VIPs often prefer to fly by the seat of their pants rather than wrestle with such figures as

$$\text{Annual duration per person} = \frac{\text{No. of days lost in a year}}{\text{Average population at risk in a year}}$$

or

$$\text{Stability rate} = \frac{\text{No. of employees with 12 months service now}}{\text{Total number employed a year ago}} \times 100$$

It can be argued that there is nothing intrinsically wrong with the report topics or the statistics mentioned *as such*. But there is no justification for the costly production of such information when it is not used.

The problem has its roots in two places. Firstly, the management of the organisation does not know what it needs to know and is unable to understand it when it is produced. Secondly, personnel departments, having produced something, feel that their job is done and their costs are justified.

This brings us back, full circle, to the question of profit. Everything that the personnel department does should contribute to profit. Reports, analyses, statistics and so on should be produced in response to a perceived *need* and to enable management to act more effectively. The work should be

(a) Relevant.
(b) Understandable.
(c) Presented 'aggressively' with the profit aspect clearly explained.

Ideally the management of the organisation, working within a corporate plan, will know what it needs and demand it. But this is not always the case, so the personnel people must take on the job of seeking out what is relevant and, if necessary, shoving it down the throats of management.

One personnel manager argued that there was nothing he could do to influence profits. This is nonsense. High morale and well motivated staff can result in more and better quality output, which can result in improved profits. A personnel manager can contribute in the following ways:

(a) By ensuring that a fair and understandable salary and wage system exists.
(b) By ensuring that potential managers are trained as leaders *before* being appointed.
(c) By fighting for policies which encourage a sense of security.

The personnel manager can, in addition, show by means of

manpower plans how the organisation can have the right people at the right time: not too many (inflating the payroll), not too few (resulting in lost opportunities), and also avoiding the wrong type (untrained) to meet the needs of the time.

If all else fails, he can, in common with the bosses of other 'cost centres', ensure that he is not himself overstaffed and does not otherwise waste money. This is a direct contribution to profit – without any preceding investment.

But a word of warning to the managers of 'cost centres'. Don't imagine that you can quickly and easily gain acceptance of your ideas. Managements in general are so used to the notion of your type of department as an unavoidable overhead that anything creative may come as a shock.

Office administration

Personnel work is not the only business function which illustrates the point concerning attitudes to profit. Other service functions to which the same principles apply have been mentioned and a real-life story concerning office administration adds support to the argument. The story particularly underlines the role that everyone can play in 'selling the firm' – or not!

The secretary of a senior executive of a large company was expecting the arrival of an important Middle Eastern client. Her boss, Mr Supervip, was hoping to negotiate a substantial slice of profitable business with the visitor.

The visitor arrived on the ground floor of the building to be intercepted by a commissionaire who knew how august was Mr Supervip. Mr Supervip did not see any casual rag-tag and bob-tail visitors! The Middle Eastern caller asked how he could find Mr Supervip when the commissionaire (deeply suspicious) sternly replied that the visitor should take a seat while enquiries were made. A call was put through to Supervip's secretary who paled with shock on hearing the immortal words, 'There's a geezer dahn 'ere' 'oo finks e's got an appointment with Mr Supervip.'

Had the commissionaire been trained to treat all visitors with courtesy, had this visitor been ceremoniously handed over to a receptionist or secretary, had he been made to feel welcome and important, then the sale would have been started even before Mr Supervip met him. It should be added that the commissionaire in question was not a member of the Corps of Commissionaires – he was in fact a reject from the post room.

By getting reception (and switchboard) right the office services manager can increase sales. Or, he can lose sales.

If you still need any convincing that a hard look at administration and its cost (and what it contributes) is worthwhile, consider how much of your total expenses is accounted for in this way. A survey carried out for the Institute of Administrative Management showed that, in the companies sampled, overheads were as much as 39 per cent of total costs. Such a proportion demands not only a rigorous and sustained effect to control the overheads but something tangible in return for them.

Action checklist

1 Ensure that all work done in the company is profit-oriented.

2 Seek and implement ways to cut your own costs, then publicise the results. Point out in your publicity what your savings are worth in terms of sales. For example, a saving of £10,000 is equivalent to sales of £125,000 where pre-tax sales profits are 8 per cent. It can take a lot of work to generate sales of £125,000 and it can be worth saying so.

3 Train your own staff in (i) communication technique, including how to 'sell the company', and (ii) business management, and how profits are created.

4 Ask top management what it needs. The answer may

well be a blank stare of amazement, so be ready with some suggestions. Be ready to demonstrate the link with profits. Plug away remorselessly. With any luck one or two successful projects will give you momentum and you have arrived. If not, keep up the 'drip of water on stone' technique.

5 Identify work which leads nowhere and contributes nothing and get rid of it.

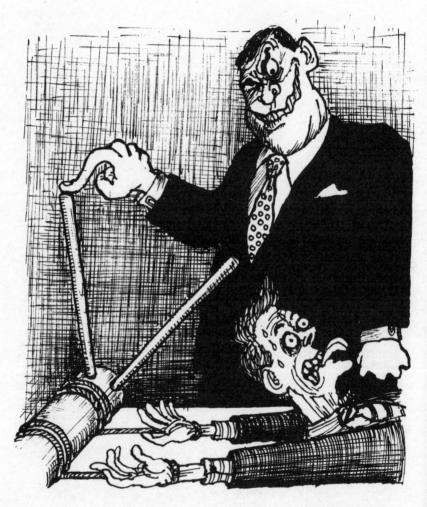

8

THE MANAGER AND PERSUASION

Analyse any manager's job and you will find that it includes
a lot of persuasion – and being persuaded. Managers have to
persuade their own staff, perhaps to accept (enthusiastically) a new bonus scheme, new equipment, different
working hours or whatever. We have to persuade customers
to buy, bankers to lend, colleagues to co-operate and wives
to accept that the new blonde and glamorous secretary is
merely another employee.

Failure rate tends to be high and more often than not new
schemes go ahead in an atmosphere of grumbling and
resistance, passive or otherwise. Some good ideas never get
off the ground at all. Some go ahead successfully and with
the enthusiastic support of staff.

In fact where the people are keen on an idea, they will
make it work even if some of the detail has been skimped or
there are flaws in the system. Since it is vital for a manager to
achieve a good score rate in his attempts to persuade, it is
worth examining the reasons for failure and success. Observations of the successes and failures of managers and executives over the years – mainly selling new ideas – seem to
indicate that the following are the key factors:

1 The idea (or object) must not conflict with the *personal*
   objectives of the person to be persuaded (persuadee) and
   ideally will support them.
2 The idea must be clearly understood in all its aspects and

'open to inspection' to remove any suspicion of hidden factors.

The obstacles to selling an idea are these:

1 The idea conflicts with an objective held by the persuadee.
2 The persuadee fears some sort of loss on his own part – not necessarily obvious or even directly connected with the idea.
3 The idea, although a good one, is not seen *by the persuadee* as relevant to his situation.

Some real-life examples will illustrate these points.

Case 1 Cloudy chicken soup

For eighteen months the management at Comfy Trusses Ltd had tried to implement some changes in a factory. There was implacable resistance from Evan, a relatively junior but influential member of staff, and general reluctance all round.

Perhaps in desperation, a consultant was asked to examine the problem. His first conclusion was that the proposals were good ones both for the firm and the employees. He discussed the proposals with Evan, who gave the consultant a series of glib reasons why the scheme would not work, but none of them had any substance when examined unemotionally. He realised that Evan was the key to the problem and that he was very effectively influencing everyone else.

By sheer luck the consultant discovered the answer when talking to one of Evan's colleagues over lunch in the factory canteen. The conversation went something like this:

Consultant: I cannot really understand why Evan is so opposed to the scheme.
Colleague: It's a bit of a joke really.
Consultant: What is the joke?

Colleague: A few bloody chickens holding everything up.

Consultant: Chickens! What on earth have chickens to do with it?

Colleague: Evan keeps chickens as a little business on the side. To do this he needs to have working hours which suit the feeding times for the chickens. This scheme means that on alternate weeks he has to come in very early and on those days his chickens will starve!

The consultant couldn't believe his ears but careful enquiry supported the story. He therefore rewrote the scheme, leaving Evan unaffected in terms of working hours, and showed him the draft. Evan expressed his delight and congratulated the consultant on producing a much better idea (actually it was 99.9 per cent unchanged) and gave his support. The idea went ahead with no more trouble.

The problem all along had been an idea which conflicted with a man's personal objective. But the objective was secret and he could not mention it.

Case 2 The personal touch

John managed a clerical department keeping records of orders placed, stock, deliveries and the like. Charlie approached John with an idea which Charlie thought would improve accuracy and save time. John did not agree and sent him away with a flea in his ear and the clear understanding that he thought the idea was about the most stupid he had heard yet.

Charlie sat at his desk and sadly pondered the injustices of the world. He knew his idea was a good one. Why should John be so dense as not to see it?

A little objective thinking made him realise what the problem was. It was himself! He was not suffering from BO or dandruff but he had put the idea to an intelligent man entirely from his own point of view. Not once had he mentioned John's wishes or welfare, so why should John make a change? Certainly not just to please Charlie or to make change for its own sake!

Charlie then wrote down the *real* benefits to John as an individual. (Writing out the benefits is, by the way, a very useful exercise. Sometimes an idea offers no benefits to the persuadee and the blank sheet of paper is a warning to think again.) He went back to John with a 'new' proposal which stressed the advantages to him. John accepted and implemented it.

Equipment salesmen fall into the same trap, with the variation that they stress cost saving as the benefit from buying. 'With this machine, Mr Snooks, you will reduce wastage costs by 10 per cent.'

Fantastic! (providing Mr Snooks cares a jot about wastage costs). The fact is that Mr Snooks may only be interested in saving costs if that helps him to achieve some other objective, such as pleasing his boss or winning a political point. Unless it is Mr Snooks's *own* money being saved, he is probably not the slightest bit interested.

A cynical view? Certainly, but how else do we explain a refusal? The salesman has quite a difficult task to find out (by questioning and discussion) what *will* persuade Mr Snooks. It could be as simple a matter as overcoming Snooks' fear of selling the same idea to his own boss. An offer of help from the salesman may be all that is needed.

The manager can face a whole range of other obstacles to persuasion, including the following:

1 *Fear of losing status.* This is a sensitive area and the manager can expect opposition if the change means someone losing status or status symbols. These can include an office on the 'executive floor', a personal secretary, or a seat on a committee.
2 *Fear of losing a perk.* Prestige travel, company cars, use of the executive dining room and Christmas presents from salesmen all mean something to someone.
3 *Fear that the idea will be difficult to sell to staff.* The persuadee

may himself see difficulties in convincing his own staff, and he may lack the confidence to try.

4 *Fear of ulterior motive.* The idea could be the thin end of a wedge of terrifying proportions and type.

Note that so far all the obstacles mentioned are based on fear. This is best dealt with by consultation, getting the people concerned to identify the problem, and helping them to find the solution. Too many managers lack the will or confidence to do this. Some regard it as a loss of face or status. Such managers suffer the consequences in the form of opposition.

5 *Tradition.* 'We have always done it this way.'

6 *Poor explanation.* The persuadee is not really sure what it is that is being suggested. He may also have been given an incomplete explanation and he is filling in the gaps with his own pessimistic assumptions.

7 *Implied criticism.* The proposed scheme may be replacing one the listener designed in the first place. Alternatively, he may feel that there is dissatisfaction with his perform-ance – hence the new approach.

8 *Alternative idea.* The persuadee may have some ideas of his own and he feels annoyed that they have not been asked for. Even if the persuadee has no alternative idea, he can be upset by not being consulted. Sometimes very upset.

9 *Lack of choice.* As in the case of a fait accompli, everyone suspects a 'choice of one option'. Some variations on the theme from which people can select (and reject) makes them feel more secure.

10 *Personal problems.* Domestic problems, ill health, financial worries, drug-taking children and the like can all turn a normally reasonable person into a 'difficult personality' who will reject even the most reasonable and modest proposal.

One of the great difficulties in dealing with these obstacles is spotting them in the first place. Very rarely will anyone promptly tell you that they lack confidence, have status worries or are upset by the wife's adultery with the man next door.

The solution again is the one too many managers neglect –
consult, discuss, consult, discuss until *together* a solution has
been found. Above all make sure that there *are* benefits for
the persuadee and that he is aware of them.

The money persuader

The use of money – or goods – as a means of persuasion
deserves special mention, since there is no doubt that some
men can be bought. For proof of this, keep an eye on the purchasing department during December. Salesmen who
hadn't a hope of seeing a buyer during the rest of the year
will be welcomed at Christmas present time.

Alternatively, try getting a telephone installed in certain
countries. A bribe means you can have it now. No bribe, no
'phone.

However, there is one thing that money will not buy –
enthusiasm.

Humphrey was a senior executive who, having taken over
a new job some three months before, was indulging in an
ego trip of massive proportions. He was the great 'new
broom' sweeping away everything in sight – including
everything worth keeping.

One of his best men (Dick) had just resigned and Humphrey realised that he had gone too far. He asked the personnel
manager to talk to Dick to persuade him to stay on. Dick was
not in a mood to be persuaded. His reason for leaving was
that the new boss was an arrogant bully who was changing a
happy and effective environment into a miserable one. He
had destroyed the interest of the various managers by reducing their authority and responsibility and Dick had no desire
to carry on.

The personnel manager reported all this back to Humphrey (in unvarnished terms) with a recommendation that he
talk to Dick himself (and the other managers) and admit that
he had 'misjudged the situation'. This suggestion was more
than flesh and blood could stand and after some huffing and

puffing Humphrey declared that every man has his price. He called Dick in and offered him a massive increase in pay. Dick accepted and stayed on. Six months later he left and the personnel manager met him to discuss the matter.

Dick stated that the increase in salary had been more than he could resist but his lack of enthusiasm for the job (and the boss) was such that work became a misery. He decided to leave after all, and, ironically, obtained a job with an even higher salary!

The point is a simple one. It is possible to buy a man's presence in your firm but it is not possible to buy his enthusiasm. That must be earned through good management.

There is an added danger that in using money to persuade an unhappy man to stay on a manager may implant in the organisation a sullen, silent enemy. Such people can be a threat to the stability of the organisation and, in a subtle, even unconscious, way, can sabotage the operation. However, when a manager is so bad that he has to resort to bribes to keep people, there is probably not much left to sabotage!

In fairness it should be said that there are quite a lot of managers who sincerely believe that money motivates. Perhaps it is the definition of 'motivate' that is the problem. It is certainly true that underpayment can actively discourage. It is not necessarily true that overpayment can actively encourage. It seems likely that in certain special cases, such as heads of mighty industries, money *will* motivate – not for its intrinsic value but for what it represents. Thus, when a government offers a very highly paid man an even higher salary to run a nationalised industry it is, in effect, making a public statement of his status and esteem. He doesn't need the cash and much of the increase will go in taxes. He *does need* the status symbol of a high salary and it is the status that motivates.

There is one more situation in which wages and salaries should be considered. Like Dick, who had to be bribed to stay on, employees working for a poor leader tend to seek higher pay. If there is little or no enjoyment to be gained from the job, and no prospect of moving on, the employee will seek more money as compensation for his misery.

Sometimes employees will be pushing for pay well above the market rate. When they don't get it, the misery is reinforced and management/employee relations go down the drain. If they do get more money, production costs go up and the firm becomes less profitable and/or less competitive. Either way the bad leader is an expensive character to have around.

The business of persuasion

There are, in addition, various general factors which experience suggests are important in the business of persuasion. In summary it seems that to be successful the persuader must:

1 *Appear attractive.* An appearance which is attractive to the audience (e.g. dressed in the same way) gives an impression of credibility and trustworthiness. It is not an accident that film villains are portrayed as overdressed, dressed in black, of foreign origin, grossly fat, etc. Any physical appearance contrary to the fashionable norm creates feelings of mistrust – even revulsion.

2 *Include both sides of the argument in the statement.* This draws the teeth of the would-be opponent and also confirms that the persuader is being eminently fair and reasonable.

3 *Keep the story consistent and simple.* Any change of direction will destroy credibility. Complicated arguments require concentration and hard work to follow. Presenting the other man with hard work and mental exertion will not endear you to him.

4 *Be persistent.* If at first you don't succeed . . .

5 *Present the case in the most effective order.* The early and later parts of the message will have most impact. The impact of the message can be further enhanced by arousing fear in

the listener. The fear to be aroused is that of the awful consequences of *not* accepting the idea on offer.

Try this sequence:

(a) Explain the advantages to be gained from a new idea (linked to personal objectives).
(b) Describe the idea, in a nutshell.
(c) Point out the losses to be suffered if the status quo persists.
(d) Repeat the advantages – in brief.
(e) State the idea again – in a very small nutshell.

6 *Choose the right medium/situation.* The effectiveness of a message is much influenced by choice of method. The following methods are placed in descending order of effectiveness:

(a) Face to face on his territory.
(b) Face to face on neutral territory.
(c) Face to face on your territory.
(d) Films, slides or pictures.
(e) Tape recordings.
(f) Written messages.
(g) Messages sent via a 'go-between', e.g. secretary, assistant, shop steward.

Note: A face-to-face presentation on the other man's territory, *backed up* by films or other visual aids, is a very powerful combination.

Examples of the wrong approach can be seen in many of the brochures produced by companies to sell themselves or their products. One made a not untypical attempt to make the written word more effective by adding pictures. This brochure of some twenty-five glossy pages opened with an inside cover photograph of the chairman.

There sat this captain of industry in all his glory. His benign smile (probably never seen by his employees), combined with his greying temples and earnest expression, were no doubt intended to give an impression of reliability, integrity and profound wisdom. Unfortunately, it gave no indication of the products on offer. Potential customers may have been led to think hard about profit margins when they viewed the elaborate and expensive office furniture and general display of opulence.

The next nine pages were similar. Not until page 10 was reached was it possible to discover what the company did! The brochure treated the reader to photographs of the impressive head office, the board of directors round the board table (all looking very earnest and alert) and splendid pictures of a variety of scenes ranging from a golf course to a factory.

Page 10 yielded the information that the company was a financial institution and, slowly, the services were outlined. Unfortunately, the reader would by then be too bored with pictures of golf courses, factories and earnest executives to bother.

Action checklist

1 Study 'sales technique' and put it into practice.

2 Don't expect ideas to be *willingly* or *enthusiastically* accepted. Find out what the obstacles are likely to be and deal with them first.

3 Look at the problem from the other person's point of view.

4 Be cautious in the use of money as a means of persuasion. It may be easy to buy the man but difficult to buy his enthusiasm.

9

THE MANAGER AND MEETINGS

In the March 1982 issue of *Management Today*, Hugh O'Neill wrote an article on meetings in which he reminded the reader of the opposing views that meetings are a waste of time and that meetings are essential. This is a problem for managers. All managers have attended meetings which have achieved nothing, meetings with no clear purposes, interminable meetings, boring meetings and meetings for the sake of it.

O'Neill described a situation where it was shown that on the days that managers in a certain factory held meetings productivity dropped, owing to a lack of available managerial manpower to make decisions. One might well argue that the very purpose of meetings is to make decisions, but there are the decisions required on the spot (i.e. at the work place), when machines go wrong, raw materials run out, employees go sick, disputes break out, etc., and these decisions, vital to keeping output going, cannot be made by absent managers bogged down in a lengthy meeting.

The size of the problem can be considerable. Imagine a small company of say 100 people. There may be five directors, ten managers and fifteen supervisors. If these senior would-be decision-makers spend respectively 2 hours, 1 hour and ½ hour per day in meetings, there is a total of 27½ man/hours when on-the-spot decisions cannot be made — per day!

You may disagree with the figures quoted. If so, work out

how much time your own managerial force is tied up in meetings and form your own conclusions as to how significant it is. Experience suggests that many 'shop-floor' workers are held up far too long, far too often, because the boss is at a meeting. It is obviously worth keeping an eye on the frequency, necessity and length of meetings and holding them down to the minimum.

O'Neill goes on to give his ideas on the essential requirements to be met in holding a meeting, e.g. to make a decision or to produce a plan. Further interesting and useful advice is given in the article, which along with other publications provides us with all the advice we need. There are many books available on chairmanship, agenda setting, minute writing, etc., and a good film by Video Arts ('Meetings Bloody Meetings'), all of which can help.

There is no need to attempt to summarise or duplicate all this advice here but there are some additional and worthwhile comments based on consultants' observations over the years. They too have been bored, exasperated and depressed by meetings, but, in common with everyone else, have to accept that meetings are at times unavoidable.

The most fundamental observation is that individuals change when they are present at a meeting and are, at the time, *a member of a group*. The phenomenon is much like the familiar one of putting a normal, sane, responsible man behind the wheel of a car. He can become a lunatic – irrational, unreasonable, ill-mannered, even suicidal.

Exactly the same phenomenon occurs when individuals are placed in groups, but it is harder to see it. If a speeding motorist crashes into a wall, the event is highly visible. If the members of a group ignore a sensible course of action and choose a poor one, the fact may not be apparent for a very long time.

However, despite the lack of dramatic visibility, the *group* can take a suicidal action which no *individual member* of the group would have taken when acting alone. In other words, meetings can be damaging and dangerous as well as boring and pointless. This is due to the existence of something which psychologists call 'Group Think' – the way the collective mind of a group will work.

Group Think is not easy to spot at first but becomes more obvious when the symptoms of it are spelled out. They are particularly visible in a group which has met regularly over a long time, e.g. a board of directors. The symptoms are as follows:

1 The *group* believes it is always right. There is one director who, at board meetings, regularly agrees with the rightness of decisions taken but equally readily changes his mind on the train going home. (His colleagues find him very tiresome.) His change of mind takes place when the effect of being a member of the group has worn off. Having spent some time in solitary cogitation, he doubts the rightness of the decision which he happily accepted when in the safety of the group.

2 The *group* believes it is invulnerable. All members consciously or subconsciously divest themselves of any *personal* responsibility and thus become uncaring about attacks from outside forces. The *group* therefore assumes a feeling of invulnerability, which is the sum of the individual attitudes.

3 The *group* believes that anyone who opposes it is a crook and the personification of evil.

4 There are always present in the group one or more 'sentries' who ensure that any challenge to group norms or traditions are nipped in the bud.

Judging by the memoirs of politicians, cabinet meetings exhibit all these features to a marked degree. They may be seen in business meetings which also demonstrate the *effects* of the group mentality, which are the following:

1 The group when given a number of courses of action to choose from tends to latch on to one of them very quickly.

2 Alternatives are readily ignored and drawbacks to the chosen course are understated or not stated at all. This is most marked when the chairman of the meeting is the big tycoon running the business. (Everyone agreed with

Adolf Hitler, however bad his choice of action was. The history of the Russian campaign illustrates this point very well.)

3 Outside advice is not sought. There is a variation on this theme which can be seen from time to time. Outside advice is sought as a matter of 'good practice' – with the firm but unstated intention of ignoring or rejecting it. In one such case outside advice to the effect that a newly emerging competitor was a danger to be taken seriously was rejected as ridiculous. 'They are beginners in a tough market and haven't got a chance,' said the chairman. Six years later the competitor was dominating the market (and is still expanding rapidly).

4 Evidence is sought to support the chosen course of action. Any evidence contrary to the chosen course is suppressed or ignored.

5 The reactions of outsiders are not considered, or are played down. These reactions include those of unions, employees (no, the two are *not* the same), newspapers, competitors and customers.

The manager must obviously guard against these situations, but, since we are all human and subject to group influences, this is not at all easy. We will all, at our next meeting, slip readily into the comforting womb of the group. The familiar and comforting surroundings of the conference room or boardroom will insulate us from the harsh realities of the outside world. The warmth and security of mutual agreement between the group members will dull the critical senses. The harmony of the group must not be disturbed by dissenting voices (unless carefully muted) and awkward questions avoided.

Thus, like the car driver cut off from reality by a shell of metal and glass, we will proceed towards our suicidal end metaphorically gripping the hands of our colleagues. Individually we are not responsible, so we can accept the security of the group womb and close our eyes to the nasty facts of life. After all, collectively we must be right.

If all this sounds like eyewash, take a hard look at the meetings you attend, especially the routine ones. Are they all characterised by objective analysis of clearly stated problems? Are clear decisions reached after careful and complete consideration of the alternatives? Do all the participants really contribute or do the majority merely go along with the vociferous minority? Do you have a sneaking feeling (which you are reluctant to admit) that most meetings are a waste of time?

What then can be done to improve the quality of meetings and the decisions taken? The following 'rules' should be followed:

1 The chairman must adopt all the techniques of good chairmanship, which have been described in numerous publications and need not be repeated here. In addition he must look for and stop any 'Group Think'.

2 The status or personality of any one participant should not be allowed to cloud the judgement of the others. For example, one group of people was, for some four years, dominated by one member. He was the oldest, not the most senior in rank, but had the strongest personality and loudest voice. Unhappily he was not the brightest.

3 Try to divide tasks so that each member can take an active part, e.g. by carrying out some research and reporting results to the meetings.

4 Tailor the size of the group to the size of the problem. Superfluous people are not only a waste of manpower but an encouragement of Group Think.

5 Vary the type of people in the group. When all the participants are lawyers or accountants or salesmen or whatever, the approach to problems will be distinctly one-sided.

6 Ensure that there is a common goal – which is clearly stated and understood.

One group of executives (which achieved nothing of any significance over many years) was, when faced with the question, quite unable to decide what it was responsible for. One of the members of the group took to one of the meetings a list of topics which he felt the group should actively deal with. The group, very happily and willingly, not only rejected them all but was then unable to agree on even one subject that it *was* responsible for! Yet the meetings continued!

The members of another group, closely observed over a number of months, seemed to concentrate their efforts on congratulating each other. Votes of thanks appeared in the minutes. Congratulations were voiced at each meeting. This was undoubtedly a very pleasing social scene but little ever emerged to make a scrap of difference to the business.

7 Make sure that the members of the group are really competent to handle the subjects under discussion, for they will tend to trivialise the difficult subjects to suit their own level of competence. This is the only way that people can cope with work above their level, and it is much easier than admitting ignorance or incompetence.

Action checklist

1 Avoid neglect of the business by too many meetings. Keep your officers in the front line as much as possible.

2 Beware becoming a victim of 'Group Think'.

3 Follow Rules 1–7 above.

4 See Appendix 1 for a source of helpful advice on how to run meetings (if you *must* have them!).

BIRCH AFTER DELACROIX

10

ANARCHY, REBELLION AND LEADERSHIP

When Sir Michael Edwardes took over BL (now the Rover Group) in November 1977, he faced, among others, two major problems. One was an ageing product line and the other was a bloody-minded workforce. The workforce was, it seems, led by local union dictators rather than by management, which seemed to have given up, only too anxious to take the line of least resistance. The result was a dying firm – uncompetitive, unproductive and only kept alive by injections of the long-suffering taxpayers' money.

Four years later Edwardes had achieved a great deal on the industrial relations front. Man hours lost through disputes fell from about 15 million in 1977 to about 1 million in 1981. Output per man was improved, with a 30 per cent increase in one year alone.

It is not unreasonable to hope that with a competitive product line appearing on the market at competitive prices the company will return to profit and expansion. Jobs should be created and the taxpayers might even get some of their money back.

What was Edwardes' style? Obviously it is worth studying and drawing lessons from it. It seems to boil down to a very simple formula:

1 Find out the facts.
2 Decide on objectives.
3 Explain the facts and the objectives to the workforce (in plain, down-to-earth language).

4 Tell the workforce what the plan is.
5 Implement, and stick to it come what may.

Items 3 and 4 in the above list are particularly important and those which are most often omitted or neglected by too many managers.

The fact is that a true leader will communicate with his team and give them the *facts*. A number one failure in management is to assume that the workforce are too stupid to see what the facts mean. Managers particularly shy away from communicating unpleasant facts.

The vast majority of people are able to understand the facts of life and will rise to the occasion when they face trouble. Providing that the plan for dealing with the problems is realistic and logical, then the good leader can expect support. Failure to inform the workforce not only insults them but also has the following drawbacks:

(a) It allows them to assume that the manager has an ulterior motive, is dishonest, about to perpetrate a con trick or whatever.

(b) It allows a politically motivated union boss to exploit the assumptions and fears of the workforce.

The workforce, if fully in the picture, will not be so stupid as to allow themselves to be exploited and damaged by union bosses. They will even, as happened at BL, run these characters out of office. The manager can then get on with the job of building the future *with* his workforce.

If anyone doubts the wisdom of telling people the bad news (many managers *do* have this doubt), they should take a lesson from Winston Churchill. In the early stages of the last war when Britain faced invasion and defeat, Churchill promised 'Blood, sweat, toil and tears'. He did not promise a politician's Utopia – and the people backed him.

On a personal level the same phenomenon can be seen in the reluctance of managers to carry out an appraisal interview with a 'bad employee'. It is no great hardship to conduct an appraisal interview with a keen, successful employee. The whole event can be an occasion for considerable pleasure both for manager and appraisee. But to go through the agony of obtaining agreement on the weaknesses of a poor performer, and agreeing on constructive joint action to improve matters, can be daunting. This is the very case, however, in which appraisal is most valuable. To obtain recognition of inadequacies and to identify the solutions is a big step forward both for employee and employer.

Experience suggests that the unsatisfactory employee will rarely fight against fair comment, however unpleasant. The poor performer's thoughts are likely to reflect the following reactions:

(a) Thank heavens that the difficulties I am facing are coming into the open at last!
(b) What a relief to be able to discuss my problems!
(c) This appraisal may give me a chance to find a solution to my problems.
(d) At last someone is taking an interest in me.
(e) The uneasy atmosphere in which I have been working is getting me down. Now the air will be cleared.
(f) This gives me a chance to explain my worries and aspirations.

Of course, the poor performer *will* fight if he knows that the appraisal interview will be nothing more than a sterile 'telling-off session'. Such a confrontation is not a true appraisal at all, although, sadly, many managers think it is.

Managers should not be afraid to discuss problems with their staff openly. It is far better to talk it out than brood over it, to do something than let things fester month after month.

The key is to have some solutions to offer − something constructive and tangible to discuss so that a plan can be jointly constructed to turn a poor worker into a good one (and a good one into a better one). Such action benefits both sides. Above all, if an employee is not performing to his manager's satisfaction, he has a right to know. He then has the option of finding another job if he cannot see any future where he is.

Sometimes a manager will find his whole department slipping from his grasp. One of the most dramatic examples of anarchy occurred in a clerical department.

Terry, the manager, was responsible for a group of twelve clerks who prepared and processed various documents before their passage to the accounts department. The accounts department had many complaints regarding the quality and quantity of the work and an O & M analyst, George, was asked to examine the systems.

The systems were fine (in theory) and George decided to examine the methods for control of the work, output levels etc. It was soon obvious that output fell dramatically every Friday, and George discovered that there were always at least two clerks absent on each of those days.

He spoke to Terry about this and after some pressure Terry shamefacedly admitted that in addition to Stella, who was pregnant and attended a clinic on Fridays, one other of the clerks was allowed a day off on a rota basis. This had resulted from a demand from the two supervisors, who had expressed the group view that if Stella was allowed a day off each week, then it was only fair that everyone else had a day off. (Even if they did not have to attend the ante-natal clinic!)

In fact, having obtained Terry's agreement to this arrangement, the group had extended it such that about 20 per cent of the workforce could be missing at any one time. An elaborate but entirely unofficial recording system had been set up and, each morning, the fifteen-minute tea-break had been extended to about an hour while agreement was reached on who would be absent and when. The relative merits of shopping expeditions, social activities, long weekends to visit the continent, etc., were evaluated.

Further enquiry revealed other 'shop-floor' practices, which explained the lack of output and generally poor quality work. The supervisors had completely taken over from Terry, who spent most of the time in his office with the door shut. Terry knew that he had lost control and eventually admitted that he was afraid of his staff and afraid to take a firm line.

George had every sympathy for Terry. Any young manager could have been overawed by the people in his charge.

The problems were discussed at length but no amount of persuasion could get Terry to put a stop to the unreasonable practices. He repeatedly expressed his fear that if he made a fuss, the clerks would resign or, worse, just ignore him. In George's view a few resignations would have been ideal, as there was no doubt that with proper control of work a satisfactory level of output could have been achieved with considerably fewer staff.

Eventually George concocted a plan. He would present to Terry and his staff a new set of operating methods which would cut across all the existing practices. The methods included regular and routine reporting to Terry, who would parcel out work. The supervisors would be required to support this control within a framework of records which they would maintain. Having made his presentation and assuming executive powers which he did not possess, George then announced that all days off (except for genuine illness, etc.) were cancelled, that tea-breaks would be limited to fifteen minutes and sundry other absences would cease.

The reactions were as follows:

1 A stunned silence for about sixty seconds.
2 A loud and angry protest from one of the supervisors, who publicly threatened to resign (George publicly offered to accept her resignation).
3 A series of mini-meetings (mostly in the loo) to discuss things.

Little work was done during the rest of the day and at 4.00 pm Terry called them all together and, now much encouraged, gave the following message:

1 Everyone had 'got away with murder' and had now been rumbled.

2 The changes would be enforced.
3 Discussions would be held with staff on details of the changes and their co-operation in implementation would be welcome.

This was greeted with sullen silence. Finally, the supervisors were interviewed and told (by Terry) that their co-operation was hoped for but if not forthcoming, their resignations would be accepted.

The next day a series of discussions with the staff were started on the details of the plan and, apart from having to enforce the tea-break, which again showed signs of prolongation, Terry had little trouble. Gradually the atmosphere improved. The staff showed every sign of enjoying the chance to contribute to the detail of the working methods, and the supervisor who had threatened to resign did so. This supervisor had clearly been the ringleader, and, seeing the staff respond more to Terry than herself, felt too embarrassed to stay on. Eventually Terry found himself back in the driving seat and the desired objective of improved efficiency was achieved.

This was a case of announcing the changes before any consultation or involvement of staff – contrary to the advice given elsewhere in this book. George might have done better to consult first, but it is doubtful. This was one of those cases where things were so bad that a severe jolt was needed to break up a well entrenched set of attitudes. Once this was done, the consultation process followed successfully.

There was a fascinating post-script to this little saga. About a year later George was talking to one of the clerks, who referred to the supervisor who had resigned. 'We hated her,' she said, 'she was too bossy'.

Action checklist

1 Treat your workforce as intelligent people by giving them all the facts, good and bad.

2 Talk problems through with employees. Ask for their views and ideas. Take them into your confidence as much as you possibly can.

3 Manage firmly, fairly and openly.

BIRCH

11

THE PERFECTIONIST MANAGER

There are managers who proudly proclaim 'I am a perfectionist'. Some go on to explain with smug satisfaction that mistakes are 'not tolerated' in their departments and that none of their staff would dare to produce anything but perfect work. Some go even further with nostalgic comments about standards and values of the good old days (the 1930s?) and refer to the days of copperplate entries in calf-bound ledgers as if such methods were practicable in the 1980s. On the face of it to strive for perfection is a praiseworthy ambition and it is extremely difficult to persuade the perfectionist manager that he is, in fact, wrong.

The difficulty lies partly in the fact that there are many situations where anything less than 'a perfect' result is unacceptable. For example, a piston must fit a cylinder within certain tolerances in order for the engine to function to the laid down specification. A container will either hold its stated volume or not. A quantity of material will either weigh a stated amount or it will not. There is little room for compromise in those 'physical situations', although even in scientific or engineering environments criteria are stated in such terms as 'plus or minus 0.1°C' or 'plus or minus 1.2 per cent'. There is in other words an acceptable working tolerance.

This acceptable working tolerance is an equally vital ingredient in the 'non-physical situation' such as price negotiations, time-keeping, report-writing, advertising design, letter-writing, estimating and work measurement. The perfectionist manager who will not accept a degree of tolerance creates the following problems:

(a) Wasted time
(b) Lost opportunities
(c) Wasted money
(d) Demoralised staff

Let us consider some real life examples.

Case 1 Urgent duplication

Rodney had taken on a new secretary who, on her first day, was given a number of tapes of Rodney's dictation to transcribe. The secretary worked hard all day and by late afternoon gave Rodney a substantial pile of letters to sign. Rodney rejected them all and insisted that they be retyped because the margins were too narrow.

Rodney had not told his new secretary what his personal preferences for layout were and she used the same width margins that she had used (acceptably) for previous bosses. Many of the letters had become urgent as a result of the delays caused by the period when Rodney had no secretary and things were now made worse by Rodney's insistence that they be typed all over again with wider margins.

With one decision Rodney lost a day of valuable time, thoroughly upset his new secretary, reduced his own productivity and probably damaged his own image. It is highly probable that impatient recipients of his letters were led to further doubt Rodney's capabilities when yet another day went by with no response from him.

Case 2 Gold-embossed perfection

A brochure was prepared describing the company's new product. Various drafts were produced, checked and rewrit-

THE PERFECTIONIST MANAGER   109

ten until, finally, the approved version went to the printers. In the fullness of time, and after much nagging (the brochure was of course now *very urgently required*), the printer delivered 5,000 beautiful glossy copies.

Everyone was delighted except Mr Graymatter, the managing director. Mr Graymatter had noticed a spelling mistake – in the index. His horror at finding the word 'introductory' spelt 'introductery' was so great that he ordered the whole brochure to be reprinted.

The cost was substantial and the delay such that the brochures were not ready for launch date. It is likely that the extra cost and the value of business lost were very much greater than any losses which might have resulted from the spelling mistake (probably nothing).

Case 3 The price for Stanley

Stanley was in charge of the pricing department. He had a small team of young men and women whose job it was to calculate prices to be quoted for the service which his company provided. The output of the department was poor and quotations were often so badly delayed that by the time they were ready the customers had gone elsewhere. A consultant was asked to examine the problem.

The consultant found that Stanley, who prided himself on his reputation as a perfectionist, had laid down a procedure for calculation which had the following features:

1 A great deal of small detail, which could only be obtained from the customers, was required. The resulting questioning irritated the customers and caused lengthy delays.
2 The detail appeared to be irrelevant both to staff and customers, resulting in lack of confidence in the system.
3 Every calculation had to be double-checked by Stanley. This not only doubled the time for certain parts of the work but further delay was caused when the work joined a pile on Stanley's desk waiting for his attention.

4 An excessive degree of 'accuracy' was imposed by an insistence on work being carried out to two places of decimals. This was in spite of the fact that some of the basic figures were *estimated* (guessed) by the customers!

The consultant found that the staff were petrified of making an arithmetical error and did the work over and over again before summoning up enough courage to present it to Stanley. Should Stanley find an error his wrath knew no bounds and the unfortunate employee was further reduced in confidence by the acidity (and duration) of the tongue-lashing he received.

A more rational method of calculation was worked out by the consultant, who found a compromise between a two-minute scribble on the back of a bus ticket and a two-day agony of calculation and recalculation. The problem was not solved, however, until Stanley was moved to another job. When that happy day arrived, a newly motivated staff got on with the job in a commonsense, workmanlike fashion. Productivity went up, sales increased and profits improved.

Case 4 Too late for action

There are many other examples of the costly struggle for perfection. An unusual one was found in a certain hotel in a European city which employed a clerk to check all the bills, after the guests had departed! This resulted from a substantial under-billing which occurred some years before, causing a state of panic and apoplexy in the management. Whenever the clerk found that a guest had been undercharged, the manager wrote a letter to the guest asking for the balance of the money.

Examination showed that the cash result was negligible for the following reasons:

(a) There were a number of false addresses. Mr Smith was not likely to take chances that his wife (Mrs Thankins) would find out where he had been.

(b) Guests who were now safely in their home towns hundreds or thousands of miles away were not too concerned about the possibility of writs or extradition for a few pounds.

The clerk also checked the bills presented to diners (again, after their departure). This was to ensure that the waiters did not undercharge by mistake. Since any losses were deducted from the waiters' salaries, they made a point of overcharging, which, from time to time, caused some monumental rows in the restaurant.

The hotel manager had never queried the cost or value of the checking but justified it on the grounds of perfectionism. It is likely that some staff training would have been a good substitute, possibly in combination with an occasional spot check.

There is one other point worth making about the perfectionist manager. His staff will do all they can to hide errors rather than risk their necks by revealing them and sorting them out. This can result in hidden errors 'bouncing' much later, when the damage has been done. Staff who have no fear of admitting the occasional and inevitable error are more likely to put them right.

Action checklist

1 Be cautious about striving for perfection. Perfection is expensive – go for excellence instead.
2 Review standards of working. Are they unnecessarily high? Are they illogical?
3 Review checking procedures. Do they achieve anything worthwhile? Do they actually worsen the situation? For example, does your company check all the bills received? The chances are that most of them are machine-produced and contain no arithmetical errors. Analysis will probably show that checking bills below about £50 in value is not worth the clerical cost.
4 Decide on some acceptable working tolerances. If they are properly explained, your staff will not abuse them.

12

THE MANAGER AND HUMOUR

The value of a sense of humour should be stressed as a 'tool of management'. Management should of course be treated seriously but not necessarily solemnly. There is some amusement to be gleaned from many of the situations in which managers find themselves.

One such was the case of Mr Dimblebum, who was *very, very* important. Mr Dimblebum was head of a large purchasing department with a budget of many millions. He had a huge office, two secretaries, and a carefully developed aristocratic manner. Furthermore, he was the terror of his staff.

One of his company colleagues (Albert) was engaged in the reorganisation of the purchasing department and was given the job of drawing the organisation charts for publication. Albert had described Mr Dimblebum on the main chart as 'Controller, Purchasing'. Mr Dimblebum was most displeased and pointed out in severe tones that his title was 'Comptroller, Purchasing'.

Albert slunk away, tail between legs, to find a dictionary. His delight was complete when he read the dictionary definition of Comptroller – 'Mis-spelling of Controller'.

Many happy moments were enjoyed debating whether or not Mr Dimblebum should be advised of the definition. There was much happy speculation on how he should be told and what his reaction would be. In the end everyone thought better of it and Mr Dimblebum duly became Comptroller, no doubt to his great satisfaction.

A quite different situation arose concerning two departments heads known by their staff as Tweedledee and Tweedledum. Dee and Dum for short. These two gentlemen had disliked each other for many years and their enmity was a company institution. They communicated only by a third party and were endlessly finding fault with each other.

This state of affairs became a particular problem when their joint help was needed in implementing some new systems. They were both in favour of the new ideas but neither would discuss them with the analyst responsible if the other was present. Somehow a way had to be found to make them friends, or at least put them on speaking terms.

Dee was a keen rose grower who told the analyst one day that he was in need of a load of horse manure but was appalled at the cost of it. Dum, the analyst knew, rode to hounds and might perhaps have some horse manure to dispose of. So it turned out. Dum quite readily agreed to let Dee have some horse manure and Dee, although a little surprised, was pleased to accept it. Having negotiated the exchange, the analyst left the two men on speaking terms — both in fact showing signs of relief that peace had been achieved without loss of face on either side.

A week later a visitor walked into the office to find Dee's staff and Dum's staff looking out of the window, speechless with laughter. They pointed out of the window to the scene in the car park below. Dee and Dum were standing by their cars, red-faced and exchanging abuse at the tops of their voices.

It transpired that Dum had brought some horse manure to the office in the boot of his car. He was in the act of transferring it to the boot of Dee's car when Dee appeared. Dum, being a horseman, was not averse to a little horse manure here and there but Dum most certainly was. The fact that Dum had carefully placed a sheet of plastic in Dee's boot was not enough to convince Dee that this was not a deliberate and most unfriendly act and confirmed his old view that Dum would always be his enemy. Dum in turn felt that Dee was (quote) 'An ungrateful bastard'.

THE MANAGER AND HUMOUR

All the careful negotiating had come to nothing but the other employees did have some hilarious lunch-time discussions as a result of it all.

Dee, by the way, emptied the manure in his boot on to the car park and suffered the further indignity of having to move it when the works manager complained. Apparently he moved it, in the dark, when everyone else had gone home.

Another favourite story concerns Fiona, who was secretary to a VIP. She was about twenty-five years of age, very beautiful and very haughty. Wherever her boss went, she went. Not only did she accompany him on business trips, to conferences, lunches, etc., but she joined in all discussions on every topic. Her boss doted on her and no one dared to object or argue when she put forward even the most ill informed views.

She would make dogmatic statements on investments to the finance experts, on production to the factory managers, on salary schemes to the Personnel Director and so on. Fiona was heartily disliked and a nuisance to everyone.

No one knew what to do about it until one day the company was visited by an expert in office design who had been commissioned to examine the office accommodation. He joined a group for a working lunch and there, of course, was Fiona. The visitor was clearly puzzled by Fiona's presence and found it difficult to place her among the various executives present. He was also obviously put out by her frequent comments and was very clearly not prepared to allow Fiona to tell him his job. His irritation became more and more apparent and Fiona finally received her come-uppance.

The visitor mentioned a painting by Toulouse Lautrec, which he had seen in someone's office. 'Toulouse Lautrec,' said Fiona excitedly. 'My parents know him well!' 'Presumably,' said the visitor, 'the secret of your expert knowledge, acquired at such an early age is spiritualism. Even *your* parents would find it difficult to know a man who died 100 years ago.'

Not even Fiona's boss could ignore this remark and she never appeared again at managerial gatherings.

One more cautionary tale is worth recording. This story concerns Ben, a buyer.

Ben was a great exponent of the art of squeezing Christmas presents out of sales representatives, and during the month of December he had a steady stream of visitors bearing expensively wrapped packages. His staff were not allowed to share the booty and, understandably, were none too enthusiastic – particularly when Ben would display the gifts and expect their admiration.

One day a salesman called, presented his package and departed. A few minutes later a furious Ben emerged from his office loudly telling his secretary that the salesman would never be allowed in the office again. He angrily stated that the man was a disgrace to his calling and the company would have no further dealings with him.

The startled staff were delighted to discover that the gift was a pair of hair brushes. Ben was almost totally bald!

13

THE PROFESSIONAL MANAGER

Roget's Thesaurus places the word 'professional' alongside 'past master' under the heading 'Proficient'. This definition provides a good pointer to the direction in which every manager should be heading.

While perfection in management is so unlikely as to be a negligible prospect (and probably undesirable – see Chapter 11), every manager should seek proficiency. Attainment of proficiency must not be restricted to one or two aspects of the job but must embrace the whole range of skills, techniques and attitudes required to be truly effective.

First and foremost, managers should concentrate on improving their abilities in dealing with people. Difficult situations when viewed from the other person's position are often made easier to deal with. Even a few seconds' pause for thought before making a response to a statement can convert a potential long-term conflict into a profitable constructive relationship. Concentration on what really matters will achieve results, whereas struggling up to the neck in a swamp of pointless detail often leads only to the psychiatrist's consulting room.

Concentration on profit and how it can be achieved is an essential activity. Analysis of a problematical situation in terms of profit can often make the decision easier for the manager. For example, the answers to the following 'acid-test' questions will frequently indicate the action to be taken:

1 If I owned the business, what would I do?
2 Does the proposed idea contribute to profits?
3 Can we do as well without taking the action being considered?
4 What alternatives are there and have they been evaluated?
5 If I do nothing, what will the company lose?

Above all the professional manager avoids attitudes such as 'I will look at this when I am less busy' and 'I think we should hand this over to the accounts department'.

The more senior the manager, the more important it is that he broadens his technical and financial knowledge. The senior man should be well able to see beyond one department's boundaries – even beyond a division's boundaries in a large organisation. He or she should be able to match the specialist in at least the basic concepts of the specialist areas and be able to take a decision confident that the essential facts are understood.

Chief executives should be clear about their role, and all their colleagues should have an equal understanding. The CE must stick to this role and not waste time and money fiddling about with the work of others. Apart from everything else, the CE who works to his job description will receive more support and loyalty from his team.

All of this presents a daunting picture of what the professional manager must achieve. There are two saving graces. Firstly, if anyone successfully achieves it all, that person will be the world's first (and probably last) perfect manager. Secondly, every situation has its funny side, although, admittedly, this can often only be appreciated some considerable time later. However, if all else fails, the professional manager can fall back on his sense of humour. It's a lot cheaper than hospital bills and funerals!

APPENDIX 1

Sources of help and ideas

One of the vital needs of the manager is to locate the answer to his difficulties quickly. The answers should be as brief and simple as possible, and, with one exception, the suggestions for reading and viewing which follow meet those criteria.

The chief executive who wishes to review his role, and possibly that of the whole board of directors, could do worse than to read *The Board of Directors and Effective Management* by Harold Koontz (McGraw-Hill). This book at 275 pages is the longest of the items of reading matter that will be suggested. In view of the importance of the CE's job the time and effort should be worthwhile.

Koontz defines management as he sees it in terms of the directors of a company, and covers such topics as the functions of a board, decisions to be made, areas of control, operating methods, etc. He devotes a chapter each to the roles of chairman and chief executive, and, perhaps most valuable of all, gives suggested job descriptions for these positions.

Also useful for the CE (and his subordinates) is a very readable 64 pages in *Leadership is not a Bowler Hat* by Peter J. Prior, published by David & Charles. The author is chairman of Bulmers, the cider company, and the contents reflect his personal ideas on leadership. Some of the ideas are controversial (and thus more interesting) and should provide food for thought at all levels of management.

Top Management Strategy by Tregoe and Zimmerman (John

Martin Publishing) is also easy reading and, at 128 pages, not too long for a business trip by train or plane.

Persuasion techniques for managers (Chapter 8) are provided in Antony Jay's *Effective Presentation*, published by British Institute of Management. The book is, as its title suggests, primarily concerned with the formal presentation. Advice is given on visual aids, film commentaries and the like and, although this is aimed at the big occasion more than the less formal face-to-face meeting, the techniques of putting the message across are the same.

Selling and Communications skills are also covered in a number of films marketed by Video Arts Limited of Dumbarton House, 68 Oxford Street, London W1N 9LA.

Video Arts also offers a range of films which will be useful to the manager who is keen to get on equal terms with his accountants (see Chapter 3). Titles such as 'Depreciation and Inflation', 'The Control of Working Capital' and 'Cost, Profit and Break-Even' speak for themselves. Most of the films run for about 20 minutes and it is amazing how much can be learned in such a short time. For those who require it, Video Arts provides a series of booklets, on the same subjects, giving the essential facts in doses small enough to be swallowed during the average commuter's train journey to work.

Finally, on meetings (Chapter 9), the Video Arts booklet 'How to Run a Meeting' is recommended as a very worthwhile 32 pages.

APPENDIX 2

Making your reading pay off

Having read this book you, the reader, have expended some of your valuable time. I hope the preceding chapters have been interesting and that your time has not been entirely wasted. However, books on management should be more than just a source of entertainment, and having read them the reader should have gained some ideas which will improve his professional skills.

Let's assume that some useful ideas have been acquired. Let's also assume that the training experts are right when they say only 25–30 per cent of the information read in books is actually retained in the conscious memory.

Two objectives must be achieved in order to profit fully from the time spent on this book, and achieving them will involve a little more of the reader's time.

First the useful ideas gained must be applied in practice to have any real value and, secondly, the percentage of retained knowledge must be increased to say, 60 per cent (perhaps ever 100 per cent). It is not necessary to read the whole book again to raise this percentage but it is worthwhile looking at certain sections again as part of a four-stage 'improvement programme'. This programme, which follows, should also be entertaining and will achieve its objective of tangible and beneficial results for the reader.

The four-stage programme

Stage 1
Re-read Chapter 1 (The Compleat Manager) and Chapter 13 (The Professional Manager). Take particular note of the activities required for effective use of human resources and the necessary personal qualities listed on page 14 plus the skills mentioned on page 15. Then look again at pages 119 and 120.

NB. You will notice, on page 120, the exhortation to avoid saying 'I will look at this when I am less busy'; try also to avoid saying it with respect to this programme.

Stage 2
Photocopy the questionnaire which follows and put the copy in a safe place for later use. Then go through the following questionnaire ticking the boxes. Please be honest with yourself – cruelly so if necessary – as the only thing to be gained by kidding yourself is a false sense of security. Should there be any topics which do not apply to your situation skip them and go on to the next topic.

How do I rate myself?

	Entirely satisfied	Room for improvement	A long way to go
1 Understanding of the 'company' needs			
2 Co-operation with other managers			
3 Use of human resources			
4 Personal qualities			

	Entirely satisfied	Room for improvement	A long way to go
5 Executive skills			
6 Technical skills			
7 The result of the self-assessment at the end of Chapter 1			
8 Accounting knowledge			
9 Ability to 'instruct' accountants			
10 Avoidance of conflict			
11 Working attitude to the opposite sex			
12 Other (non-sexist) prejudices			
13 Results of the checklist to Chapter 6			
14 Comparison with the characteristics on page 52			
15 Damage caused by workaholism			
16 Contribution to profits			
17 Persuasion abilities			
18 Value of meetings			

	Entirely satisfied	*Room for improvement*	*A long way to go*
19 Dealing with 'rebellion'			
20 Realism in handling detail and acceptance of quality tolerances			
21 Ability to see the funny side			
For chief executives only **1** Delegation			
2 Relevance of work/role to the business			
3 Understanding of *all* the company functions			
4 Indulgence/over-indulgence in the good life			
5 Avoidance of ups and downs of activity			
6 Avoidance of favouritism			
7 Value of 'state visits'			
8 Answer to item 7 of the checklist to Chapter 2			

Having placed your ticks in the appropriate columns you can now 'take a view' of your own performance. Rethink the

'Entirely satisfied' column bearing in mind that (a) this is a tough standard to achieve but (b) perfection is virtually unattainable. In other words, you can allow yourself to be entirely satisfied if you get it right, say, 95 per cent of the time. Most of your ticks will probably appear in the 'Room for improvement' column and it is a good idea to jot down the nature of the improvement you have in mind.

The 'Long way to go' column should give you food for thought and makes up most of the work to be done in the next stage of this programme. Anything ticked in this column will be, by your own assessment, a weak point demanding priority for positive corrective action.

Stage 3

Set yourself a target time of about six months to find and implement ways to improve your performance as indicated by the position of your ticks on the questionnaire. Anything much less than six months is probably too little time to achieve real improvement, and if you allow too long (e.g. 12 months) you will be in danger of:

- Becoming bored with the exercise.

- Putting things off till tomorrow, next week or next month.

- Losing sight of your purpose.

You may be in the unfortunate position of having so many weak points to work on that the whole problem is too daunting and depressing to contemplate. If so, pick out three or four of what you think are the most pressing items and deal with them – ignoring the rest until later. Dealing with the problem in small, digestible bites is an easier course to follow and frequently the most effective method.

The problem areas can be tackled in various ways and a list of them should be prepared and considered. Some problems may be better tackled one way and some another, and the following are some alternatives to choose from. It is up to you to decide which are the most appropriate.

- Re-reading the relevant parts of this book and applying the ideas in practice – for example, by using the action checklists.

- Following up the suggestions in Appendix 1 for sources of help.

- Attending *appropriate* training courses.

- Consultation/discussion with staff, colleagues and bosses.

- Consulting an expert from outside the company.

- Observing how others do it: the successful are the obvious choice but don't overlook the unsuccessful people. If you can identify what they are doing wrong you can avoid it yourself.

Don't be discouraged by failure in the early stages. A new style of leadership, delegation, avoiding conflict or whatever takes practice and uprooting the habits of years is not easy. Be patient with yourself but be persistent – there is a lot to gain.

Stage 4
At the end of the six months (or whatever period you have chosen) take out the photocopy of the unticked questionnaire that you made at the beginning of Stage 2.

Without looking at the completed questionnaire place ticks in the photocopied version, taking the same care and consideration as you did the first time.

Now compare the two versions of the questionnaire.

Hopefully, some of the ticks will have moved to the left and, if things have gone really well, there will be none in the 'Long way to go' column. If so, reading this book and completing this exercise has given you more than mere entertainment and you, your colleagues, your staff and your boss are all better off as a result.

If not, don't give up – try it again.